MILLION DOLLAR METHOD™

MILLION DOLLAR METHOD™

Grow Your Influence, Audience, & Revenue Fast!

JAMIE WOLF

Disclaimer

This book is for educational purposes only. The views expressed are those of the author alone. The reader is responsible for his or her own actions. Adherence to all applicable laws and regulations, including international, federal, state, and local governing professional licensing, business practices, advertising, and all other aspects of doing business in the United States, Canada, or any other jurisdiction is the sole responsibility of the purchaser or reader. Neither the author nor the publisher assumes any responsibility or liability whatsoever on the behalf of the purchaser or reader of these materials.

Editors: Million Dollar Story Agency

Book Design: Phillip Gessert

Cover Graphics: PixelStudio

If you're ready to scale your business to $100,000 per month and beyond and to become a published, bestselling author fast, even if you don't like to write or don't have time, we have solutions!

JOIN our FREE group, find out your INFLUENCER SCORE, & schedule a FREE CALL!

Join Our Influencer Circle Community!
https://www.facebook.com/groups/influencercircle.milliondollarstory

What Is YOUR Influencer Profile Score?
Find Out If Your Influence Is As Healthy As You Hope It Is & Where It Might Need A Boost!

Find Your Grade Here:
https://www.milliondollarstory.co/yourinfluencerprofilescorecard

Book A FREE Call Today!
Ready To Scale Your Business Using A Book As The Vehicle? **Contact Us**
https://calendly.com/milliondollarstory influencer-circle-scale-your-business

DOWNLOAD YOUR FREE
PUBLISHING PROFIT GUIDE!

This is my gift to you for buying this book

TO DOWNLOAD YOUR FREE BOOK, GO TO:
https://www.milliondollarstory.co/publishing-
guide

TABLE OF CONTENTS

ADVANCE PRAISE

KIANA DANIAL

People sometimes overlook the power of a book as an evergreen lead generator. It's organic traffic at its best—you do the work once (write your book now) and it continues working for you for years without any new effort or expense on your part. I am pleased to be a Best Selling author of multiple books because I know they are a great way for prospects to get to know, like, and trust me, thus becoming a warm audience for my offers. If you've thought about growing your brand and your business, then write a book now! Don't put it off. And if you're ready to write the right book to grow your audience, influence, and revenue, then be sure to work with Jamie Wolf and use The Million Dollar Method^{TM} she spells out in this powerful book!

Kiana Danial is a multiple best-selling published author and award-winning, internationally recognized personal investing and wealth management expert helping moms take control of their financial future as CEO & Founder of Invest Diva. Kiana is a frequent expert on many TV and radio stations and has reported on the financial markets directly from the floor of NYSE and NASDAQ. She is a weekly investment expert guest on Tokyo's #1 Investment TV Show and has been featured in The Wall Street Journal, TIME Magazine, CNN, Forbes, The Street, and numerous other publications. She is also a Two Comma Club award winner for generating $1 Million in one of her businesses.

investdiva.com

CARLA WHITE

Do you appreciate the power of a book to build relationships and nurture leads? It's organic traffic at its best—you do the work once (write your book now) and it continues working for you for years without any new effort or expense on your part. It is also a great tool to complement your other offers, going hand in hand with speaking and podcasting! I am pleased to be an award-winning multiple Best Selling author because I know books—and the media attention they bring—are a great way for prospects to get to know, like, and trust me, thus becoming a warm audience for my offers. From a business strategy standpoint, a book is something to do first—not someday! And if you want an easy and fast path to get your book written to grow your audience, influence, and revenue, then be sure to work with Jamie Wolf and use The Million Dollar Method^{TM} she outlines in this relevant book!

Carla White is a multiple best-selling published author and the Founder and CEO of *Hiro.fm*, the *Gratitude Journal* and host of *Radical Shift* and she has been featured in Oprah, Forbes, Entrepreneur Magazine, and The Huffington Post.

https://hiro.fm
https://carlawhite.org
http://thegratitudeapp.com
https://radicalshiftpodcast.com

EVANS PUTMAN

Are you looking to increase your visibility, build your authority and grow your profits while attracting your dream clients? As a frequent podcast guest, a podcast host, business coach and consultant, and a published best-selling author, I know from experience that a book will do all of that and more. Not only have my books positioned me as a more sought-after podcast guest—which gets me on increasingly influential shows with larger audiences—but they have also opened the door to opportunities to speak at events and summits. And yes, being a published author has definitely helped me grow my bottom line! Along with my non-negotiable that my clients create a podcast sales funnel, I also highly recommend that they write a bestselling book to use as an asset to grow their business and brand. And when you are ready to write your book and ensure it hits the bestseller list, be sure to pair up

with Jamie Wolf and use The Million Dollar Method^{TM} presented in her newest book! And, don't forget to check out the
bonus section to learn more about podcast book launch tours!

Evans Putman is a husband, a father, a 2X best selling
published author, a Podcast Host, Coach, & Consultant, and
Founder of **www.evansputman.com**

JAMES GOLDEN

Did you know a book paves the way towards reducing the
time it takes to convert a lead into a sale? It also smooths the
way to reducing the cost to convert a prospect into a client.
It's not a stretch to recognize that a book is a lead generation highway, leading prospects to your offer via your stories.
But until now, most entrepreneurs have not appreciated that
a book is a bridge to lead conversion and sales as well. As
you read The Million Dollar Method^{TM} you will discover that
it's possible to write a best-selling book in parallel with crafting both your front-end and back-end offers. And then drive
those offers home with a funnel that delivers all the assets—
the ebook, print book, audiobook, and even a mastermind or
course—all in 90 days while still donning all your other hats!
As a published, best-selling author, company owner, family
man, and movement builder on a mission, I know what's possible. When you work with Jamie and Million Dollar Story
Agency you will have found the vehicle to take you to your

destination and smooth roads to get you there quickly and easily!

James Golden is a best-selling published author and a respected entrepreneur, pavement preservation activist, podcast host, and speaker.

www.jg3consulting.com
www.facebook.com/groups/thegoaldencollective

MARK STERN

Every business, small or large, digital or brick & mortar, local or global, needs the same things to first survive and then thrive: Lead Generation and Prospects, Lead Nurture and Relationship Building, and Lead Conversion and Sales. If you aren't making sales you have a hobby—it may bring you joy but it drains your resources. That's why books are such a useful tool for business building. They are efficient—you invest one chunk of time, attention, and cash to send them into the world, and they act as magnets drawing prospects and clients to you. The sales conversation happens within the book! You share your stories, you paint the picture of where the reader will arrive when they travel with you, and as they consume your content, they realize you have the solution they've been seeking. Once they purchase, you have the opportunity to stand out again by instantly delivering a physical product to them that thanks them plus provides tools to get started. Custom Boxes are the Ultimate Authority in differentiating you so now you've created not just a customer but a raving fan who will stick with you and refer others to you. If you want to check boxes of raising your authority, building your brand, and becoming #1 in your market, work with Jamie and Million Dollar Story Agency.

Mark Stern is a best-selling published author and an innovation and digital strategy consultant with over ten years of experience helping Fortune 500 companies mitigate disruption of exponential technologies and realize their strategic vision. He is also the Founder of the Custom Box Agency

customboxagency.com

DR. GRACE LEE

If you are an entrepreneur who has worked hard to create, then sell, an offer, have you ever felt the fear of wondering if you can fulfill that sale? Yay! They bought something. Oy! Now, what do I do?!? Developing strong business acumen and mastering your professional destiny means, among other things, you make sure you have systems and processes in place to support your business. Writing an outline for a book puts the roadmap in place, not just for the book, but when done with strategy and intention, for your course or Mastermind, too. Know that writing a book and collaborating with other influencers for affiliate-offer upsells can systematically create assets for your entire value ladder, lets you do work once, and reap the benefit for years. For instance, both a book and a YouTube channel are distribution platforms, helping you to establish your brand authority while disseminating your content to a broader audience. People learn and consume information in different ways. Another client delivery mechanism could be video content housed on YouTube based on your book content that is the foundation for your course content. Do you see how, with the right strategy and the right systems and processes in place, you can exponentially make a difference for yourself and others? One proven process to getting your book done fast is to work with Jamie Wolf and Million Dollar Story Agency!

Dr. Grace Lee is a best-selling published author, the Founder of Mastery Insights, and Podcast Host of Inciting Influence & Career Revisionist. She has 2.4+ Million views on her YouTube channel, 10k+ subscriber growth per month, and $80k+ new monthly business revenue

tubecelebritycodex.com

CHRIS BADEN

As an expert, think of writing a best-selling book—becoming

a published best-selling author—as creating a tool in your sales ecosystem. When you strategically write the right book, it can be an SOP—a standard operating procedure—for your offer! In other words, your book outline can be the step-by-step process for your prospect to overcome the barriers and obstacles they face and it can map to your Mastermind or course. Businesses never use just one tool; they create multiple systems and processes, and select software and tools that support the results they seek. A book is an evergreen source of lead generation, a way to nurture those prospects through your story-telling, and a delivery and fulfillment system when it complements your core or premium offer. Now that you have built your brand with a book, increased your authority and visibility to attract a targeted audience, be sure to have a system to move those prospects through a pipeline as they enter your world—and a way to deliver what you promise. As a published best-selling author, a busy dad, and co-owner of a software company, I know that working with Jamie Wolf and Million Dollar Story Agency and using the right software creates a formidable sales ecosystem for your business!

Chris Baden is a best-selling published author and an experienced Co-Founder with a demonstrated history of working in the marketing and advertising industry. He is a co-founder of Sales Ascenders and a new CRM software company, Flow-Chat, and has received a Two Comma Club award for generating $1 Million in revenue with one of his businesses. **www.FlowChat.com**

AKBAR SHEIKH

As a multiple best-selling author, consultant, and winner of quite a few Two Comma Club awards, I still say I don't know how to do technical stuff. I also don't believe in hustle. They aren't my things. My whole deal is helping people make more to give more. I know that when you help people achieve huge success that allows them to give back, they feel fulfilled and they stick with you, support you, buy from you, and refer you. You move from strictly business to community, and people inherently desire to belong to a community. That's why joining a community of experts who are also published best-selling entrepreneur-authors feels great! It's why you can use a book to share stories and solve problems so that your prospects become lifelong customers. A book is a fabulous gateway to retaining and ascending your clients through your value ladder. When you succeed, celebrate! When your clients succeed, celebrate them! And then give back—and share stories about that, too! If you're like me and don't want to waste time learning technical stuff because what's important is the work you do to make the world a better place, work with Jamie Wolf and Million Dollar Story Agency to become a published best-selling author fast—and you won't even have to write if that's not your thing!

Akbar Sheikh is the CEO of his eponymous company, a multiple best-selling published author, a winner of 5 Two-Comma Club awards (and counting), a TEDx speaker, and helps coaches scale to 7-figures

www.AkbarSheikh.com

ERIC BEER

I'm all about starting conversations. And then closing them. Leads are truly the life-blood of any business. And yet, if those leads don't convert to closed sales, they won't actually keep your business alive. As a published, best-selling author, father, and business owner, I know the responsibility of getting traffic, and converting that traffic into sales, predictably and consistently. I also know it has to be cost-effective. As an athlete, I'm inherently competitive. I want to know percentages and margins. The time and money cost has to make sense. That's why I chose to write a book. It's effort you do once that yields rewards long-term. It raises your brand visibility and your authority. You are forever more recognized as a published, best-selling expert. As a member of Russell Brunson's Inner Circle I also know that networking with the right influencers can be life-changing. Working with Jamie Wolf and Million Dollar Story Agency connected me to other influencers, increased my audience reach, and started a lot more conversations!

Eric Beer is a best-selling published author, a serial entrepreneur, an investor, an expert affiliate marketer, and a digital marketer. He is the Founder and CEO of Universal Marketing Partners and the host of **Performance Marketer**^{TM}

https://www.univmp.com

KACI BROWN

Jamie Wolf is an incredible visionary who leverages her gifts and talents to bring authors' stories and lessons to life. I had the privilege of working with her on the very first Million Dollar Story book in the series. Her mission of connection and structure to work within is a joy to watch. I love that in this book she shares the exact actionable steps you can take today to make your book a reality. Becoming a best-selling published author is not only closer than you think but incredibly powerful (and needed) for many people who need the information you have. Impact absolutely reaches much farther than words on a page. Share your story!

Kaci Brown is a best-selling published author, the CEO of Amplify My Impact, a Business Consultant & Marketing Strategist, and the Host of Amplify My Impact Podcast. **www.AmplifyMyImpact.com**

TAMMY DONNELL

Jamie Wolf is a colleague who helps coaches and consultants attract new clients & sales in 90 days to become #1 in their market with increased brand visibility and authority. In the newest book released by her Million Dollar Story Agency, Jamie shows you how the process of writing a book helps clients create high ticket offers and an automated business. Forget Complexity! Lose the Overwhelm! Jamie shows you how to create assets, funnels, + traffic with just one effort in a short 90 days so you stop being stuck!

If you have expertise in a particular niche and are a coach or consultant, you may still not know how to take what you do and get it out to the market and if you are like a lot of people, you just want someone to wave a magic wand and take what you know and voila! Your business is ready to GO! That's what the Million Dollar Method is all about! I highly recommend Jamie if you are serious about growing your business!

Tammy Donnell is a best-selling published author, and an Agency Owner specializing in web development, social media, SEO, and consulting.

www.GrowthManagementAgency.com

JEREMY NICOLAIDES

Jamie Wolf is a colleague who helps experts jump to the top of their market by writing a best-selling book. This new spotlight as an authority figure raises them above crowded playing fields and makes them the clear choice over the competition. Now, in the latest book released by her Million Dollar Story Agency, Jamie reveals how you can create additional products, like courses and masterminds, while writing your book. Your new best-selling book will drive in new leads, nurture relationships, and shave time and money off your conversions. Jamie makes the process of writing a book fast and painless. She guides you to monetizing it to grow your audience, influence, and revenue as you build your brand and grow your authority.

Jeremey Nicolaides is a multi-award-winning movie industry veteran who worked on Blade Runner 2049, Transformers: Dark of the Moon, Star Wars Eps. 1-3, and Men in Black 3, and others, and has held titles including Executive Producer for Legend, Global Creative Director, Producer, & Chief Creative Director. Known for successfully collaborating with filmmakers, producers, and studios in 3D, VF, and Digital Intermediates, Nicolaides' extensive experience on both the studio and vendor side has given him a valuable perspective on cultivating and supporting relationships with creatives and clients, ensuring their projects get on screen with the highest quality possible, on time and on budget. His own company, Golden Octopillar, consults for creative companies, invests in companies that support creatives, and coaches creative entrepreneurs on building and growing their businesses so they can get to a life of creative and financial freedom as quickly as possible. **www.goldenoctopillar.com**

LEANNE WOEHLKE

Jamie Wolf is a colleague who has a goal to help you get the absolute best results for your brand and your business in 90 days or less. In the newest book released by her Million Dollar Story Agency, she shows you how her bulletproof system is all about working with you so you can scale your business from where you are now to $100k/mo by helping you build your entire business infrastructure of front-end offers, back-end offers, and delivery system while increasing your brand visibility and authority; a book is the vehicle that takes you to your final business destination and Jamie has a proven track-record helping experts get their content turned into ebooks, print books, and audiobooks in parallel with your course or Mastermind signature offer!

Leanne Woehlke is a best-selling published author and a Tony Robbins Results Coach who helps clients find and connect more deeply to their purpose. She refers to herself as Coach~Yogi~Wife~Mom~Firewalk Instructor!

www.tonyrobbins.com/team/leanne-woehlke

THOM SHIPLEY

I have been fortunate enough to get to know Jamie Wolf over the past few years. I have been impressed by her process for helping experts become best-selling published authors. Her methodology is prescriptive and has been successfully implemented by experts a number of times. One of the challenges that experts have is finding the right opportunities and establishing their credibility. One of the best tools for this is becoming a best-selling published author to build brand authority. Jamie makes the process of writing a book fast and painless and shows you how to monetize your audience.

Thom Shipley is the President & Co-Founder of Foundry Brands

www.TShipley.com

ANGELA LITTLE

Jamie Wolf is an inspiration to many entrepreneurs and she's helped many experts write their best-selling books, taking them to #1 in their market…. imagine becoming a Best Selling Author!!! In the newest book released by her Million Dol-

lar Story Agency, she shows you how the process of writing a
book brings business clarity and can even allow you to craft
your new, or next, course or mastermind in tandem with
writing your book. Becoming a best-selling published author
builds brand authority for you and your business. It also
brings you leads, nurtures relationships, shortens the conversion time and cost, and even helps create ways to deliver your
offer. Jamie really focuses on scaling your business to $100K/
month using a book as a vehicle to craft your course or Mastermind, create your front-end and back-end offers, and have
your entire business launched and generating consistent leads
and cash within 90 days!

Angela Little is the Founder of StrongWomenFitness & Creator of The "Badass Bikini Body the Complete Blueprint for
your Perfect Keto Body."

www.strongwomenfitness.co.uk

PREFACE

Imagine you are at an inflection point in your business. Perhaps you are pivoting and heading in a new, more focused direction. Maybe you've decided to rebrand or launch a new brand. Possibly you've recently decided to leave corporate behind and begin the venture and adventure that will bring you fulfillment. Or you simply have decided it's time to add another, or new, offer to grow your influence, audience, and revenue. In other words, you've committed to scaling fast.

Whether you are focused on a new revenue stream or an additional revenue stream, contemplate what that means to you, your business, and your resources of time, money, and effort: You'll need to educate your audience about what you do (now); you'll need to attract new potential customers and clients who want your solution; as an action-taker you must convert that potential into sales—realized revenue—in as short a time as possible with the least amount of resources— time, energy, money, opportunity cost; finally, not only do you need to attract and gain new clients, but you need to keep them around once you have introduced them to your world.

Well, that sounds daunting! But those five factors comprise

what I call The Profit Pentagon^{TM} and they are essential to every business.

Systems and processes are also essential to every business, otherwise you can't operate efficiently, increase capacity, and scale. If you don't scale, you aren't making the impact or creating the movement that brings your vision to life.

Take a trip into the future with me—just 90 days from today. Imagine how you will feel to see your business firing on all cylinders, thriving in each area of The Profit Pentagon.^{TM} Imagine also that you are still standing and you are confidently and clearly thriving because you used a system— a methodology—so that you worked once and produced all the results your business and brand require to grow your influence, audience, and revenue. FEEL how light, happy, amazing, successful, and energized you are now to help more people! Wow! THIS is why you are an entrepreneur! You have a vision and you find the best way to bring that vision to life. Well done!

The Million Dollar Method^{TM} is the ONE strategic tool that will check all boxes in The Profit Pentagon^{TM} in just three months and this book will show you how!

Even if you have NOT thought of writing a book because you are too busy growing your business, I invite you to think strategically and be as efficient as possible with your resources of time, money, energy, focus, and fulfillment.

Rather than think of a book as the endpoint, think of the exercise of writing a book as one that brings your ideal customer and the result you deliver to them, or for them, into crystal clear focus. Recognize a book as a vehicle that picks up cold traffic and delivers it to you as warm traffic, ready to buy from you because after consuming your stories, your prospects now relate to you and see themselves in your journey; they believe you can and will help them. Finally, conserve your time and energy by crafting your book and course or mastermind simultaneously in order to build out your entire business infrastructure of front-end and back-end offers once, within 90 days, while creating the systems and processes to master organic traffic and team building. Get out of overwhelm and busyness and scale your business to $100,000 per month and beyond!

If you want to boost your status, easily attract new customers, make more sales, position yourself as an authority quickly, and warrant premium pricing —even if you feel you are too busy or don't like to write—we have a unique proprietary system to get you results fast. If the thought of writing a book keeps surfacing but you aren't sure how to start (or finish), I invite you to join my free Facebook^{TM} group called the *"Influencer Circle."*

It's a group I share with fellow mission-and-success-driven entrepreneurs who are committed to growing their influence, status, and client base to make a more significant impact and change more lives. If you've rarely thought of becoming an author, but you are driven to scale your business to profit so you can make a bigger difference for yourself, your family, your community, and those you serve, the Million Dollar Method^{TM} is your solution to consistent and fast growth and impact.

I know you have a story and solutions worth sharing!

I believe that when you realize it's fully possible to scale your business to $100,000 per month and beyond, you will embrace the true legacy you are here to make. The Million Dollar Method^{TM} takes away the complexity and overwhelm, and gets you to results with relentless focus so you stop drowning in your business and get to doing what you love most, changing lives now. When you become a published author-entrepreneur of a Best Selling book, your book is working for you to make you #1 in your market. How? Let's revisit the components of The Profit Pentagon^{TM}—and don't worry… all of this will be explained in depth in the following chapters!

INTRODUCTION

THE PROFIT PENTAGON™: WHY WRITING A BOOK GOES HAND IN HAND WITH SCALING YOUR BUSINESS

- Lead Generation & Prospecting
- Lead Nurture & Relationship Building
- Lead Conversion & Sales
- Client Delivery & Fulfillment
- Client Retention & Ascension

Together, these five factors comprise the **Profit Pentagon™** *for every business!*

Whether you're a consultant, a high-ticket coach, or a business owner of any sort, you can't risk running out of clients and customers—so you need an optimized source of new leads. Always.

Once you've invested in attracting their attention, it's necessary to find ways to connect so that they come to know, like, and trust you. As tired as those three words may be, they remain essential for a *potential* client to become a *realized* customer.

The goal is to generate revenue and be profitable to make the impact you are here to make. This is the transactional piece. A sale must take place. The lead has to convert into a paid customer. And then...

You get to do what you love best! Run the mastermind, coach, deliver your offer—build the funnel, install the software, set up the ad campaign, ship the thing, give the speech, host the event—the possibilities are endless for entrepreneurs.

Ideally, you have systems and processes in place, a team to implement them, and the customer experience is stellar. Now that they have entered your world, purchased the first thing, and been satisfied, they have become loyal and hungry fans. They want the next thing you have, and the next, as they ascend your value ladder, buying increasingly high ticket offers. They stick around—and they gladly refer you to others.

Those others join the group of prospects and new leads. You find yourself going around the Profit Pentagon again: ...Lead Gen > Nurture > C&S > D&F > R&A > Lead Gen...

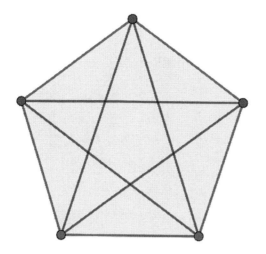

A book is such a powerful business tool that, when done right, it fulfills these five factors essential for EVERY profitable business. And doing a book right is precisely what the Million Dollar Method^{TM} covers! So let's begin!

It's been stated that Attention is the new currency.

As humans, we've long craved acceptance and affirmation that we belong.

And as humans, we're wired to share stories, using them to connect with and help each other.

The key is to make sure our stories are heard—that they get attention.

In business, we desire to amplify our Authority. We pursue that increased status by investing in masterminds to level up or expand our networks or both to advance our attractiveness.

Suppose I could show you a methodology that uses story-telling to exponentially increase your ability to Attract Attention and Advance your Authority, raising brand Awareness of your offers, resulting in your increased Affluence. Would you be open to either learning how to implement it yourself or getting it done for you?

The Million Dollar Method^{TM} uses a vehicle to get you to your desired destination.

The vehicle is writing a best-selling book and the unique secret, the magic, is using the book contents to map out and create your course or mastermind while simultaneously—almost effortlessly—producing all the assets for your entire business infrastructure.

You arrive when you become a Best-Selling published author, and you experience fast growth of your influence, audience, and revenue.

Writing a book goes hand in hand with your business strategy because it raises your Influencer Score. Remember SWOT? Strengths, Weaknesses, Opportunities, Threats? The Oxford Dictionary defines the noun 'Influence' as "the capacity to affect the character, development, or behavior of someone or something, or the effect itself." Your influence, depending on how significant or underdeveloped it currently is, can be a strength and an opportunity, or a current weakness and threat if a competitor's influence outshines yours.

The fantastic news is there are many ways to improve your influence; some take more time and effort than others. Becoming a published, best-selling author or co-author is a stealth tactic for significant gains fast! If you're curious how healthy your Influencer Score is today and want to identify which areas you could improve, get your scorecard here— **https://www.milliondollarstory.co/ yourinfluencerprofilescorecard**

Russell got help writing and publishing his books because that is not his core area of expertise, and he's otherwise engaged running a multi-million dollar company. He said at the time of writing his first book, "Not only did publishing a book help me strengthen relationships with existing customers, it got me into new markets that were previously unavailable to me.... It [sic] broke down walls, built up new relationships, and grew my business in ways nothing else had been able to do.....my brand expanded even more, my business continued to grow exponentially, as well as my ability to serve my customers at the highest possible level." Russell Brunson, Founder, Click-funnels

Russell recognized and proved to himself that writing a book (or several books) goes hand in hand with scaling your business and your brand authority—and making a difference in your community.

THE ADVANTAGES OF AUTHORING WITHIN A COHORT OF STRATEGIC ENTREPRENEURS

- Comfort food...
- Home...
- Tropical vacation...
- Book...

Each of the above words and phrases instantly conjures up images and brings up emotions for everyone who hears them. Yet my version of 'comfort food' or 'home' could be vastly different from yours! It's the same for the word 'book.'

If you've "always had a book inside you" or if people hear your stories and often say to you, "You should write a book," or if you've lived and learned and now feel compelled to share your experience as a cathartic exercise, then a book may conjure up images of your seeking a remote location with hours spent writing and rewriting something very personal to you.

You may be someone who has started but never finished writing a book. Or someone who's never started because you believe it would be years before you complete the project. You simply don't have the bandwidth or time to make it a priority. At the same time, you focus your energies on growing your business.

Of course, I'm speaking solely about non-fiction books in the business and self-development space, not the greater book universe, including fiction, children's literature, academic textbooks, cookbooks, and so much more!

There are various book types: "pocket" books, product pamphlets, books that complement eCommerce, and digital-only books used as lead magnets.

Million Dollar Story Agency and the Million Dollar Method^{TM} help you grow your influence, audience, and revenue fast because we use your book as a powerful tool to build your Profit Pentagon^{TM}.

The result is that you become a published best-selling author.

Simultaneously, you develop your influence and your relationships with colleagues, prospects, and clients.

Your opportunities expand significantly through one or more of the following:

- Increased press exposure—magazines, radio, tv, and more
- Invitations to podcasts
- Invitations to summits
- Invitations to speaking events
- Opportunities for affiliate work, joint ventures, and possible partnerships

Your audience reach multiplies instantly while you now have an evergreen lead source to grow your list rapidly.

Your brand both grows and becomes more substantial.

The book is simply the vehicle that takes you to these destinations. When I teach you to write a book, the book is almost inconsequential—all by itself.

The Million Dollar Method^{TM} shows you how to scale your business from where you are now to $100,000 per month and beyond, using a book as a vehicle.

Million Dollar Story Agency has a done-for-you program for becoming a published best-selling author if you want these results with less than twenty hours of your time and effort invested (less than 10 hours if you choose to co-author,) and you want your book available for sale within 90 days.

It is what the book does *for* you, your brand, your list, your business, and your influence that is the emotional image I want you to see and feel when you hear me say 'book.'

Got it?

The **Million Dollar Method**^{TM}**,** as described in this book, is the methodology we use to help our clients create high ticket offers and an automated business. Forget Complexity! Lose the Overwhelm! We give you assets, funnels, plus traffic so you stop being stuck!

We help you scale your business from $0 to $100,000/month and beyond!

Are you ready to attract new clients & sales in 90 days to become #1 in your market with increased brand visibility and authority? If so, stop saying "I have to do X (build my website, launch my podcast, host a summit, run a challenge, finish my course, etc!!) first before I can do anything else"—*even when you know you have already been trying for* **YEARS!**

Why?

Our goal is to help you get the absolute best results for your brand and your business in 90 days or less.

If you have expertise in a particular niche and are a coach or consultant, you may still not know how to take what you do and get it out to the market.

If you are like a lot of people, you just want someone to wave a magic wand and take what you know and voila! Your business is ready to GO!

THAT'S WHAT WE DO!

Our **bulletproof system** is all about working with you so you can **scale your business** from where you are now **to $100K/mo** by helping you build your entire business infrastructure of front-end offers, back-end offers, and delivery system while increasing your brand visibility and authority.

I keep repeating this information because it is the key differentiator between your having a hobby or having a business—or more crucially, it determines if you have a business that's bleeding you dry or a business that's wildly profitable. I know which one I want you to have so I will say it again: Every business must focus on five facets which we call The Profit Penta-gon^{TM}...

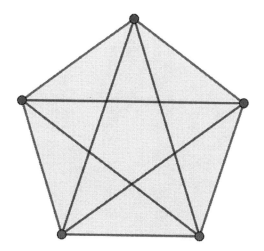

- Lead Generation & Prospecting
- Lead Nurture & Relationship Building
- Lead Conversion & Sales
- Client Delivery & Fulfillment
- Client Retention & Ascension

The problem is...

- You lack clarity and feel overwhelmed
- You have ideas but don't know where to start

- There's so much to do, you lack focus & get distracted
- You are SO busy you don't have time to build your Signature Mastermind or Core Offer
- TBH, you procrastinate or chase shiny objects
- You aren't directing your energy towards ONE RESULT

We help coaches **close any gaps** in their Profit Pentagon – **1)** Lead Generation & Prospecting **2)** Lead Nurture & Relationship Building **3)** Lead Conversion & Sales **4)** Client Delivery & Fulfillment & **5)** Client Retention & Ascension, **using our proven Million Dollar Method**^{TM} plus organic traffic methods and software.

3 Months From Today, How Will You Feel If -

- That thing you've been trying to do by yourself is DONE!
- ALL of your business assets are COMPLETE & SELLING!
- You have a PROVEN inexpensive traffic system in place
- We show you how to build your team so you aren't alone
- Your messaging is on point so you can scale fast

- You are only directing your energy towards ONE RESULT
- Your stress level is DOWN & your SALES are UP!!

We will show you how to create front-end offers plus your core offer for your Agency, Consultancy, or High-Ticket Coaching, based on the book we help you write, to **SCALE YOUR BUSINESS** in just **90 days!**

We Will Walk You Through Every Step...

- So you have complete clarity on your endpoint
- So you know what to do first, then next
- We will give you templates
- You do not have to start from scratch
- You will always know exactly what to do next
- You will start selling immediately
- You will have everything else complete in 90 days!

If You Are Past Ready To SCALE Your Business & Go Faster...

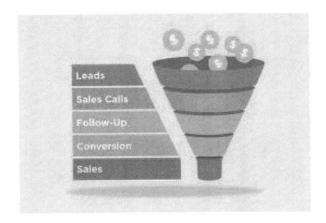

We have your SOLUTION!

In just 90 days we turn your business into a sales machine—you will have ALL of the following DONE!

- Asset #1 > Your free lead magnet (your ebook)
- Asset #2 > Your Free +Shipping book offer (your print book)
- Asset #3 > Your bump offer (your audiobook)
- Asset # 4 > Your front-end funnel is done
- Now you are prospecting organically & have ads paid for
- Asset # 5 > Your back-end funnel/core offer is done (your course or Mastermind with modules/weeks mirroring your chapters)
- Your team & systems are in place & you are set to SCALE!

- You are a Best-Selling published author—if you choose to take your content to the next level!

When you know exactly what big result you help your clients get, you easily create…

- Lead Generation & Prospecting
- Lead Nurture & Relationship Building
- Lead Conversion & Sales
- Client Delivery & Fulfillment
- Client Retention & Ascension

THE ADVANTAGES OF BEING AN AMAZON BEST SELLER

When your child plays sports, why do you care if they get a trophy or a ribbon?

When your brick & mortar first opens its doors, why do you want a ribbon-cutting ceremony?

When you got married, why did you want a wedding?

Why do parents and grandparents flock to high school and college graduations?

You can be great at a sport without needing validation offered by a trophy. You can make your first sale without any acknowledgment from your local Chamber of Commerce. You are legally married as soon as you sign the paperwork and pay the fees. And once you complete your required credits, you've earned the diploma without any pomp and circumstance.

Sounds deflating, doesn't it, not to recognize and celebrate the milestones?

We earned that trophy, that opportunity to celebrate, the moment to be recognized; a book we wrote and published is available for sale. But it's hitting and making a big deal about the milestone that draws attention, is attractive, and draws people to the event and you, which raises awareness by a lot!

Millions of new titles (books) are published EVERY year. You are an entrepreneur and business person first and an author second. Everything you do has a strategy behind it.

You want to make a difference, a more significant impact, and create a movement. You need prospects that convert to customers who stay with you, buy all that you have to offer, and sing your praises. But your efforts are hindered if the market is unaware of you and your offer. That's why you spend tens of thousands of dollars on advertising each month. It's why you host events, attend conferences, do guest appearances on podcasts, join summits, submit articles, network, and are diligent about building your brand and growing your expertise.

Becoming a published best-selling author transitions you from expert to authority.

It lets you rise above the crowded playing field.

It quiets the noise and puts you in the spotlight.

As soon as you become a published best-selling author, you are **forever** a published best-selling author! And your book stays out in the world as an evergreen lead source and relationship builder!

You can publish once or more than once.

You can write your book and be featured in other books. One of our Million Dollar Story authors became a published best-selling author in one of our collaborative anthologies and became a co-author in a book with Bill Gates, Oprah Winfrey, and others! Jack Canfield didn't sell almost one Billion books by deciding to stop after producing just ONE Chicken Soup for the Soul book, right? He's authored or co-authored over *200* books!

Shine that spotlight, earn the accolade, give people a reason to celebrate a milestone with you, elevate your standing in the crowd. Become a published Best Selling author. Scale your business to $100,000 per month. We can help you do it fast and with ease!

WHO IS JAMIE WOLF, AND WHY SHOULD YOU LISTEN TO HER?

First, I want to commend you for being here, for embracing your curiosity enough to pick up this book, and for never quitting on yourself and your dreams!

I'm Jamie Wolf, and I help experts write best-selling books and use the process of creating those books to create their entire business infrastructure to scale their business to $100,000 per month and beyond.

I help **YOU** become a best-selling author!

I help you **BUILD** your **BRAND** with a **BOOK**—or build it up even **MORE**!

Perhaps even more significantly, I make sure you write the strategic book that addresses all five factors in the Profit Pentagon^{TM} essential to every thriving business so that **YOUR** business thrives!

The result for you is increased influence, amplified authority, and cash flow. Basically, more eyeballs on you with a bigger audience reach, so more ways to monetize and more ways to make a difference.

You become the 'go-to' person in your niche!

I'm also a best-selling author. I own a boutique imprint, aka, I own a small publishing company, and I'm the founder and owner of a publishing and marketing agency. I'm a mom to three adult kids, a lifelong rescuer of dogs, cats, horses, birds, rabbits, and more, and an eternal optimist both despite and because of life and the lessons it has thrown at me.

I adore business because I am fascinated by problem-solving and believe we each have unrealized potential for greatness and for giving back to the world that gives us so much.

I am also a fierce advocate for people and their stories. I've spent a lifetime uncovering who I am and learning what I'm made of, and because of that effort... *I see you!* I see how much you care. I see how smart, talented, resilient, and creative you are. I want to help you connect with other notable influencers. I am here to share your stories and make sure your business scales fast so you can offer your solution today to the person who needs you today!

Here are my more standardized deets: I hold an MBA from Arizona State University, and I am the CEO and President of Million Dollar Story Agency and the owner of a boutique imprint, Wolf Tide Publishing. 100% of the entrepreneurs I've worked with have become Amazon Best Selling published authors and have stayed in the Top 100 in multiple categories for twelve or more months.

If you want to make more sales and position yourself as an expert quickly—even if you are not a writer—we have a unique proprietary system, the Million Dollar Method^{TM}. It features you strategically as an Influencer to multiply your audience and list with no extra effort while instantly boosting your credibility and sales; it's like you're getting a commercial during the Super Bowl!

If the thought of writing a book keeps surfacing but you aren't sure how to start (or finish), I invite you to join my free Facebook^{TM} group called the *"Influencer Circle."* It's a group I share with mission-and-success-driven entrepreneurs who are committed to growing their influence, status, and client base to become #1 in their market, to make a more significant impact, and change more lives.

Even if you feel you can't write or don't have time, I can help you! One way to get that Blue Checkmark on IG and FB without carving out too much time—**so you can boost your**

status, easily attract new customers, and warrant premium pricing—is to become a Best-Selling author. I'm guessing you have a story worth sharing!

I have been fortunate enough to have a long and varied professional journey, having worked extensively in science and business. I merged the two fields when I co-founded a medical tech and disease management company that got a product through FDA clearance in less than two years while raising millions of dollars from outside investors.

Over a lifetime of work—so far—I've experienced the roles of student, employee, corporate management, consultant, tech start-up co-founder, syndicated columnist, author, publisher, real estate investor, and owner of a boxing gym. What emerged from those experiences is a passion for working with success-and-mission-driven entrepreneurs to help them tell their stories and significantly grow their influence, audience, and revenue, which leads to making a much greater impact.

I'm also the host of *Million Dollar PIVOT*, a podcast you can catch on iTunes and other podcast sites. Hear powerful stories filled with action items as I interview entrepreneurs with stories to share that will help you believe *you've got this!*

WHO THIS BOOK IS FOR

Many of our Million Dollar Story author-entrepreneurs run at least one company generating $1M in annual revenue. Some run three or four million-dollar companies while being mom or dad of young or teenaged children. Several have earned multiple Two Comma Club awards—awards given out in the ClickFunnels community for having funnels that generate two commas—$1,000,000—of annual revenue. At least one of my author-entrepreneurs has generated over $20M in one company.

Others may not yet have monetized their businesses to that extent but have email lists and social media platform followers of 30,000 to 80,000 or more on TikTok, Instagram, LinkedIn, Facebook, YouTube, and Clubhouse.

Some of our Best-Selling authors are now multiple Best-Selling authors, recognizing the power of reaching new audiences with each new book project. They didn't say no to the next opportunity because they had previously written and published other books. Some of our authors have contributed to several collaborative works. None of our authors have limited their ability to grow their list and influence by stopping after just one book or anthology project.

Other of our entrepreneur-authors have been in business long enough to know they want to grow, they have big visions, and they work to implement them. They do not hesitate to find the solution that lets them invest in mentorship, delegation, or both to reach their goals faster. They don't ask "How much does it cost" or say, "I'll have to ask my _____" as an excuse to avoid growth. They invest in themselves strategically so they can find a way through to the solution quickly.

In a nutshell, this book is not for you if you want to write fiction, an autobiography, or a book that is in some way merely a cathartic exercise for you. You can always do those things later. Right now, your priority is cementing your brand authority and scaling your business by strategically focusing on the Profit Pentagon^{TM}, growing your influence, audience, and revenue, right?

It IS for you if you recognize you may always write a different or next book later and that no "one and done" rule exists in the world of authorship.

Right this minute, you are focused and strategic.

You see the power in becoming an author as soon as possible, writing a strategic book that brings new prospects, generates monthly cash flow, reduces both conversion time and costs, increases your profit margins, and opens the door wide to an endless flow of business opportunities.

You recognize that the Million Dollar Method^{TM} is geared towards producing content and delivering it to published Best Selling status within 90 days in order for you to cement your brand authority.

You are clear that following a framework defining what you do, where you take your prospects and clients, how they can achieve results, and who has already had success using your service or product can be described in one chapter or ten— the length is less relevant than writing NOW. You may choose to co-author at first, or you may decide to create your course as you create your book, getting twice the results with the same amount of effort. The one essential decision is that you commit to becoming a published, best-selling author now— not next year or someday!

Open up to the concept that the results you get using the Million Dollar Method^{TM} will produce a book, but that alone is not the goal.

The goal is to get more prospects into your pipeline and increase your monthly cash flow and annual revenue. You get there by multiplying your list, reaching a bigger audience, transitioning from expert to authority, and changing your brand recognition powerfully… and you achieve *those* targets by transforming yourself into a published best-selling author-entrepreneur!

You recognize that the act of writing a book brings you focused clarity on what result you provide and who your ideal client is.

You applaud efficiency and despise overwhelm so you grab onto the concept that you craft each chapter in parallel with a course module or Mastermind week.

You are SO ready to be DONE with offer creation and you are beyond ecstatic that the Million Dollar Method^{TM}, in just 90 days, creates the entire infrastructure for your business—the front-end offers (ebook, print book, audiobook), the back-end offer (your core/signature offer of a course or Mastermind), the funnel delivery mechanism, and the organic traffic methods for lead gen and turning cold traffic into warm prospects ready to buy **so that you can scale your business to $100,000 per month at last!**

If you could boost your status, easily attract new customers, and warrant premium pricing in 90 days or less with less than twenty hours of your time and effort using the Million Dollar Method^{TM}, *would you* jump on it? **Yes!**

Can you let go of the need to write the type of book that is hard to write, takes years, requires you to produce hundreds of content pages, and demands that you create and implement a marketing plan to launch it? Yes!

Then you are in the right place! You may not have revenue in the millions or an audience reach in the tens of thousands—yet! But if you see those results in your future, keep reading!

Like you, all of our authors are mission-and-success-driven entrepreneurs committed to growing their influence and impact. They know the power of relationships and networks. They start and sustain movements. They use books to move from expert to authority in their fields while partnering with other outstanding entrepreneurs.

I'm proud to call the authors—fantastic human beings who have already joined the Million Dollar Story community—my friends and colleagues. Their stories make me cry, laugh, and believe. I can't wait to welcome you into our Circle of Influence.

CAN NON-WRITERS AND INSANELY BUSY BUSINESS LEADERS BECOME AUTHORS?

I'm sure you've heard the term MVP—not Most Valuable Player, but Minimum Viable Product. The gist of getting an MVP out to the market is that great is the enemy of good, a way to procrastinate while you attempt to improve without even market-testing.

Instead, best practices encourage speed to market while listening and adjusting to feedback.

Get something out, measure results, do less of what doesn't work and more of what does work, and iterate.

When Million Dollar Story first began, we asked entrepreneurs to co-author and write ten single-spaced pages. That worked for people who liked to write but not for those who didn't.

Next, we asked busy entrepreneurs to schedule an hour for a zoom call, asked them questions, and wrote for them based on transcriptions of those interviews. That killed deadlines at the draft-editing phase. The spoken word reads quite differently from the written word—plus, they couldn't recall why they'd recounted some stories and not others. They wanted a do-over after so much had already been done.

Next, we heard from entrepreneurs who preferred to be the sole author of an individual book rather than a co-author, so we made that service available in either a completely Done FOR you offer, or a Done With You offer.

Finally, in speaking with hundreds of entrepreneurs, we heard a theme repeated often; they were pivoting, starting over, re-branding, or adding an additional business line. They absolutely understood the power of becoming a published author or writing their next book. But...

They said it would have to wait while they *first* created their new course or offer. They'd suggest we check back with them in six to twelve months. Do you know what we heard over and over again when we did that? "This has taken so much longer than I'd hoped. I'm still not done. I still haven't launched. I am still too busy to write my book."

That led to the Million Dollar Method^{TM} because writing a book and creating your core offer are not mutually exclusive! This is key if you desire a seamless way to create all your business assets in a short period of time so you can stop working IN your business and start doing what you love best which is making a difference for your clients!

The act of crafting your book around the ONE big result you deliver or the one BIG problem you solve is like magic in that it brings focus and clarity regarding your offer; you understand exactly who you serve and how you help them. As you outline each stepping stone your prospect must take to get from where they are now to where they want to be, you naturally create your chapters and course modules. By the time you complete writing your book, you also complete creating your Mastermind. Additionally you have created assets for both the front-end and back-end of your funnel and are positioned to begin selling immediately.

The exquisite result is that entrepreneurs stop struggling, stop wasting months (and months) of time, energy, and resources, and start doing what they love best—helping their clients—because in just three months their entire business infrastructure is ready to go AND they have written a book!

Now we work with exceptionally busy business owners, CEOs, consultants, digital entrepreneurs, and high-ticket coaches. These entrepreneurs hire Million Dollar Story Agency and use our Million Dollar Method^{TM} to become published best-selling authors and to grow their influence, audience, and revenue while staying laser-focused on their core business.

A very few entrepreneurs enjoy writing. None want to learn how to write, publish, and market content into best-selling ebooks, print books, and audiobooks, nor do they want to be distracted by learning how to market books. They all desire to be Best Selling published authors, reach new audiences without additional ad spend, and use yet another tool to increase their brand recognition, status, and influence easily and quickly. And if they haven't reached this metric yet, they are ready to scale their business to $100,000 per month and beyond.

We've developed a twelve-week Done With You Mastermind to work with you if you are a rising star who is ready to focus exclusively on scaling your business to $100,000 per month using a book as the vehicle and backbone to your entire business infrastructure. It's designed to move you out of busywork and overwhelm into profit in three months!

If you have already written most of your book and are ready for help with publishing, marketing, and monetizing that work, we've got a continuity program that will fit you perfectly. This is also a fantastic option if you want to re-launch a book that's already been (self-) published but perhaps didn't hit the targets you'd hoped it would. We've got you covered!

And as mentioned earlier, we do offer a full Done FOR You service for entrepreneurs who want a book written, published, and launched to Best Seller without doing any lifting, heavy or otherwise, themselves!

STRATEGY VS. TACTICS AND WHY YOU MUST PUBLISH WITHIN 90 DAYS

Strategy is the path you plan to take to achieve your mission. Put another way, it's an approach you define to accomplish an overarching outcome.

Tactics are the methods you use to move along that path. Put another way, they are tools you use to accomplish milestones that lead to that big outcome.

In *"The Art of War"* Sun Tzu wrote, "Strategy without tactics is the slowest route to victory. Tactics without strategy are the noise before defeat." In other words, a successful business requires both strategy and tactics. The first provides the map, the second involves implementation.

"Think strategically, act tactically."

For example, if you sell products and the overarching outcome, or goal, for your company is to expand market share, your strategy might be to compete on price. To fulfill this strategy, tactics might include identifying suppliers or manufacturers with uninterrupted access to resources and distribution and a track record of minimizing waste and efficiencies.

In our case, our strategy is to write a book that incorporates all aspects of The Profit Pentagon^{TM}, to produce multiple results (assets, funnel, value ladder, book) with one effort to conserve resources of time, energy, and money, and to increase our brand strength, our audience reach, and our offer price. We want to gain attention by increasing our authority. Million Dollar Method^{TM} provides the tactics to implement in support of our strategy.

THE PROFIT
PENTAGON

LEAD GENERATION & PROSPECTING

MODULE 1: DESIGNING YOUR BOOK FOR ROI & REACH

"You don't wake up to be mediocre."
Robin Arzón, Peloton

WHAT Result Will You Achieve?

The 2001 Nisqually earthquake occurred at 10:54 AM local time in Seattle on February 28, 2001. It lasted nearly a minute—a minute that felt like an eternity to me as I held my one-year-old tightly. The intraslab earthquake, meaning a slab was sinking into the mantle below, had a magnitude of 6.8. It remains one of the largest recorded earthquakes in Washington. It caused an estimated $2 billion in damage and injured more than 400 people. As soon as the ground stopped shaking, I tried to reach my two older children, but cell service was down, and it would be hours before we all made it home to discover the extent of the damage.

Fast forward seven months, to September 4, 2001. It was a beautiful fall day in New York City as I walked past the Twin Towers of the World Trade Center. I looked up at the soaring buildings where one of my brothers used to work, just blocks from where my other brother worked, and I recall thinking I was so grateful NY didn't have earthquakes. It was good to walk down that gusty narrow street and feel so safe from such a disaster...

As someone who grew up in NYC, the horror of 9/11—just one week after my walk—felt very personal. The one good thing about it was that my mom had died less than a month before it happened; she didn't have to witness or experience what would have felt to her like such a direct violation. However, with my mom gone, I soon learned how much she had covered for my father and how unwell he was.

His care fell in no small measure on my shoulders and was made almost impossible by logistics. We lived on separate coasts. I had a one-year-old as well as two older kids and a marriage that was rapidly self-destructing. At the same time, I desperately tried to hang onto a med-tech company I had co-founded. When my father died not long after my mother, all the fault lines in my own life were exposed. It was a time of massive upheaval and transition.

I don't fully recall the events leading up to my booking the call. However, I vividly remember one evening finding myself talking about all my pain with a stranger. The following day I was in an utter panic, having just spent my inheritance!

I had never heard of a "closer" before, and without fully realizing I was on a sales call, I purchased a year-long course for $10,000. It was my first investment of that scale for coaching and masterminds. Now I can't imagine not making such investments in myself regularly. However, at that time, having decided I was the most gullible fool on the planet, I attended my first event.

I was shocked when I walked into a room packed with at least 500 people; the math was pretty simple. My start-up company had raised millions of dollars from outside investors, but this was my first-ever glimpse at the business model of selling information that generated millions in revenue without giving up an ounce of company control.

WHY Does This Result Matter?

Like many of you, as an entrepreneur, I have tried a wide variety of things, chased a lot of shiny objects, and learned it takes a ton of hard work, focus, and perseverance to have a "four-hour workweek!" I've also been lucky enough to return to something I've always loved—books!

Well, more than books. People!

I love people, and their stories, and their connections, and their missions.

Plus I adore strategy and puzzles and how everything fits together.

Writing is simply a medium in which I am comfortable. Becoming published is an action, a milestone, that instantly transforms you from expert to authority in all cultures.

When I ask people why they want to write a book, I get a variety of answers: they've always had a 'book inside them,' writing their life story is cathartic, or they are hoping for a massive advance from a big publisher. If that's you, I'm not here to stand in your way. But that's not the type of book with which I help.

I've been an entrepreneur in the med-tech space. I've held the title of Director of Entrepreneurship for an Economic Development group. I've taken 100% of the authors who work with me to published Best Seller status in multiple categories in less than 90 days, all while growing their audience reach and lists exponentially. I've kept those same author-entrepreneurs in the Top 50-Top 100 in multiple categories, not for days or months, but years.

Alex Charfen identifies six core phases in your business: prospecting/lead generation, lead nurture, conversion/sales, delivery of your product or service, ascension/retention, and referrals. Once you have elevated your status from expert to known authority as a published best-selling author, the first three phases become much easier because people feel they know you, you stand out, and they are drawn to you.

Ryan Deiss says the same thing a bit differently: "A new prospect must be INDOCTRINATED before they will engage with your message; they must ENGAGE before they will buy; they must buy before they will ASCEND; and once the process is over they'll need to be SEGMENTED based on interest before they become RE-ENGAGED and buy again."

A final lens on all this is profit margin. The adage is that you can only increase revenue in four ways: sell something; sell it more frequently, sell a higher-priced thing, and sell to the same customers to reduce new customer acquisition costs. It's not good enough just to make money. You want to keep more of what you make to have healthy profit margins. One proven way to do so is to elevate your brand to increase perceived value. The athletic shoe has done this exceptionally well. Another way is to increase your average order value; once they have entered your value ladder, keep them there and ascend them to your higher-level offers. Charge a premium—which you can easily do when demand has increased and you have successfully elevated your visibility and authority. And finally, increase efficiencies by automating and systematizing as much as possible. Work one time—create all the assets for your front-end funnel, your core funnel offer, and your upsells, all while having a system in place for evergreen lead gen, lead nurture, and customer retention. Powerful strategy and results under one cover, literally!

For example, let's say you are in the fitness space, you look lean and shredded, you are a certified trainer, and you have some loyal customers… the reality is you still aren't any different from all the other well-qualified personal trainers, gym owners, or conditioning coaches. That does not diminish your knowledge and accomplishments. Still, the business landscape is filled with people with your expertise.

Strategically, you want to stand out. You don't merely want to be an expert. You want to raise your status and increase your authority. You can use different tools to do that. You can write a blog or create a YouTube channel and be obligated to feed the content beast indefinitely.

Or you can have an ad spend of thousands, if not tens of thousands, of dollars per month to buy attention that hopefully translates into influence and brand authority.

Or, you can host a podcast and invite influencers.

Or, you can host a summit and invite influencers.

Or, you can become a published Best Selling author alongside other influencers.

Or...

You can author or co-author a book AND... pursue any other paid or organic reach you choose!

It's important to note that becoming a Best Selling author is one attribute that will help you become a certified celebrity on Instagram and Facebook, earning you the Verified Blue Check Mark!

YouTube and Facebook are hungry platforms demanding to be fed content frequently. It takes time, effort, and resources to stand out in a crowd, and you still may not achieve your desired results.

As a podcast host, you can invite others and simply ask relevant questions. As the host of a ranked podcast, you become a known influencer by association with your elevated guests. Of equal importance, you have broadened your distribution because your guest will share the episode with their audience, instantly expanding your reach.

As a (virtual) summit host, you can invite others and simply ask relevant questions. As the host of a strong presenter panel and by association with your elevated guests, you become a known influencer. Of equal importance, you have broadened your distribution because your panelists will share their content with their audiences, instantly expanding your reach.

As a published author or co-author of a Best Selling book, you become a known authority figure. When you write with the Million Dollar Story community, you join fellow author-entrepreneurs who are of equal or higher reputation or are further along in business than yourself, you benefit from 'rubbing shoulders' with them. From now on, they will take your call and answer your text. Whether you hope for a warm intro to a colleague of theirs or you are ready to launch an affiliate offer or create a JV (joint venture) or partnership arrangement with one or more of them, you have built a lasting new relationship.

Perhaps most importantly, your work is launched to the audiences of all your podcast guests, your presenters, and your fellow authors simultaneously with no extra time, effort, or expense of your own, building your list exponentially while spreading your brand awareness quickly so you can make the impact you are here to create!

Before we leave the strategy of what a book does for you, I

invite you to view the idea of becoming a published best-selling author from a different perspective.

If you feel you are already an authority, if your revenue is where you want it, if your reach is broad... in other words, if you've already attained most of your business goals, perhaps you don't "need" a book.

But what if someone needs you?

Several of the authors I have been privileged to work with have chosen to participate, publish for the first time or again, solely to give back and contribute to the community. They are aware that somebody is in pain, has a problem, and is losing hope—and if their message, their story, their offer can help that person now, they feel compelled to step up and write again in either a solo or collaborative work.

They took the larger view that being a published author wasn't about them—it was about their reader, audience, and potential clients. Think of books you have read that have changed your life. You can be that author for someone!

A few of the authors who joined our Million Dollar Story community did so specifically to lend their brand recognition in support of our other authors and to give back.

That's a demonstration of authentic leadership and authority.

That can be you!

HOW Do You Accomplish This Result?

Forget about the myth that it takes two or more years to become a published author.

Forget about the myth that you only get famous in a book of which you are the sole author.

Forget about the myth that you have to be good at writing to be a published author.

Forget about the myth that you aren't good enough or far enough along to share your learned or earned experience to make a difference and an impact in someone else's life now.

Forget about the old meaning of "book" entirely!

Because you don't have to write—at all, let alone write 200 pages or more of content, you don't have to create a book proposal, you don't have to find an agent, you don't have to endure book signing events, and you don't have to store boxes and boxes of unsold books in your closet, garage, or basement!

Instead, think of becoming a published, Best Selling author with other influencers as a means to instantaneously grow and diversify your audience ten-fold with zero extra time or effort on your part, all while making new and lasting friendships with stellar mission-driven entrepreneurs—YOUR people!

Instead, focus on the result you receive when using the vehicle of a book as a means to deploy The Profit Pentagon^{TM} and raise your status from expert to authority, allowing you to attract new prospects, nurture and convert them into lifelong clients, and charge premium prices.

So how do you create a book—one more tool in your toolbelt, albeit a compelling one—that allows you to leverage micro-macro influencers to quickly reach thousands of people who need what you are offering now, not someday?

1. You create a system—or use the Trello board I've created for you (see Chapter 4)
2. You choose which facets of The Profit Pentagon^{TM} you want your book to improve for you—Lead Generation & Prospecting, Lead Nurture & Relationship Building, Lead Conversion & Sales, Client Delivery & Fulfillment, or Client Retention & Ascension. I suggest "all of them," which is covered step by step in every chapter.
3. You decide how many assets you want to create

(ebook, print book, audiobook, free+shipping book funnel, your premium course or mastermind, your organic traffic system.) You can even use the funnel I've created for you (see Chapter 5)

Let's break that down a little more, shall we?

HOW do you end up as a published Best Selling author, an authority in your space, who attracts clients on an evergreen basis, and who can charge premium prices?

You produce content.
You publish that content.
You market that content.
You monetize that content.
You collaborate and "OP" it at each step!

Let's look at the first one—producing the content.

The first thing you are going to do is to approach this whole process strategically. You will cut your workload from 100% to 10% because you are either going to collaborate or choose a done-for-you option… OR… work ONCE to get the results of your entire business done or revamped with no extra time or effort!

Whew!

Rather than create content for all the pages yourself, collaborate (co-author) and leverage other influencers to produce content that appears alongside your content. In other words, OP it—use Other People's content. (Note, they must be fully engaged and on board with this. I am not telling you to take anyone's content!)

For instance, you might identify nine other influencers who have complementary knowledge to yours while having a similar audience of active and engaged buyers.

Take the lead and ask them to participate with you as chapter contributors and co-authors. Better yet, use the 'Book Bingo' method—A4, B1! Ask four entrepreneurs to join you, and then each of you brings one more. Now you have a total of ten author-entrepreneurs collaborating on content. (You + 4 = 5 + 5 = 10)

You could host a podcast, record the shows of influencers you interview, follow my step-by-step process (remember the Trello board!), and now you have a book's worth of content.

You could host a Virtual Summit, record the presenters you interview, follow my step-by-step process (remember the Trello board!), and now you have a book's worth of content.

Don't let content production be the thing that keeps you from moving forward!

DO be sure to include other people in the process because you don't want to be stingy with the help you offer. Your goal is to OP it again. Release content not only to your audience but to other people's audiences as well. The easiest way to do that is to partner with co-authors.

Why think about your '*dream* 100' when you can have a '*real* 10' or 20? Right? Potential is just that until it becomes realized. Those 100 are a great stretch goal, but I don't want you to wait!

You are a rockstar. You know five rockstars. They know rockstars. It's a fun and powerful opportunity to fill a book with five to ten co-authors and make magic happen!

But you do NOT have to co-author or collaborate in an anthology product to save your resources of time, money, and effort.

First, let me be clear. You do NOT have to actually WRITE content if writing is a barrier for you. For whatever your reasons, if the thought of writing is the thing preventing you from sharing your valuable content in book form, as they say up North, "Get ovah yaself!" (Translation—Get over yourself. :))

There are plenty of ways to get what's in your head, the vision you see clearly, onto a written page.

Next, what final results would you like to achieve? If you want to build out your entire front-end low-ticket funnel, we've got you covered. If you want to build out your premium course or mastermind, we've got you covered. If you want 80-90% of your value ladder, including a traffic source, completed in the next 90 days, we've got you covered! We can show you how to strategically write a book that creates all your assets and delivery with one focused effort. You can do this and leapfrog your brand and your business ahead of the competition in the next three months!

WHO: Kiana Danial! Case Study Success!

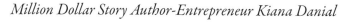

Million Dollar Story Author-Entrepreneur Kiana Danial

Let me highlight a member of our Million Dollar Story community. Kiana Danial, CEO of Invest Diva (**www.investdiva.com**), is an award-winning, internationally recognized personal investing and wealth management expert. Having been featured in The Wall Street Journal, TIME Magazine, Fox Business, CNNi, Forbes, TheStreet, Nasdaq, Cheddar, 77 WABC Radio and 710 WOR Radio, Kiana is a highly sought-after commentator, professional speaker and executive coach who delivers inspirational workshops and seminars to corporations, universities and entrepreneurial groups. Kiana has reported on the financial markets directly from the floor of the NYSE and NASDAQ, and was named the Personal Investment Expert of the Year in 2018 and the Investment Coach of the Year in 2019 by the Investment Fund Awards. An accomplished author, Kiana's books include 'Invest Diva's Guide to Making Money in Forex,' published by McGraw-Hill in 2013, 'Ichimoku Secrets' self-published in 2016, 'Cryptocurrency Investing For Dummies,' published by Wiley in 2019, 'Million Dollar Moms: Mom Entrepreneurs Share Secrets of Building Businesses & Raising Highly Successful Kids' published by Wolf Tide Publishing in 2020. Invest Diva's mission is to empower and educate women to take control of their financial future by investing in stocks and other online assets. Kiana is a 2 Comma Club earner, a mom to an active toddler, and someone we are so grateful to have as part of our Million Dollar Story!

LEAD NURTURE & RELATIONSHIP BUILDING

MODULE 2: USE MICRO-INFLUENCERS FOR MACRO LEVERAGE

"You are both a work in progress and a masterpiece."
Robin Arzón, Peloton

WHAT Result Will You Achieve?

I graduated from high school and started college when I was 17, but I had no idea what I wanted to be when I grew up. I begged my father to let me take a year off between high school and college. His response was, "Absolutely not!" which has always bummed me out because I'd found a fantastic job researching and protecting wolves out West.

I spent my freshman year of college going through the motions because I didn't know why I was there or where I wanted to go with my education. Then I dropped out when I got pregnant with my first child. My father was livid, and yet what influenced me a few years later to return to school wasn't his wrath—it was the offer of some free cake.

I'd found a job at a factory and, after roughly a year of employment there, was told there would be free cake at someone's retirement party. So I followed the food. Halfway through the frosting, it dawned on me that the woman had been there... Her. Whole. Life! Suddenly I couldn't return to school fast enough!

I've always loved animals, so when I re-enrolled in college, I decided to go pre-med, which allowed me to apply to veterinary school. As a science major, I became eligible for a work-study program with the National Institutes of Health. I worked for a Principal Investigator named Diane, who eventually introduced me to a gentleman with a fantastic job opening at a big pharma company nearby.

As a young mom who hadn't yet graduated from college, I never would have had that interview without a warm introduction. I've never forgotten that lesson—it is your network or Rolodex, along with healthy doses of work ethic, integrity, and kindness, that opens doors and provides opportunities!

WHY Does This Result Matter?

In the next module, we will cover how to write a book using content from your podcasts, your summits, or simply from co-authoring with influencers. Here's the thing...

Most people can pay attention to a book that's about 200 pages long. The rule of thumb said if you could get on a plane on one US coast and finish reading the book by the time you got off on the other coast, that was the right book-length.

One page double-spaced is about 250 words. So the average 200-page book is somewhere between 50,000 to 60,000 words. I like simple math; when you divide a 200-page book by ten authors, each author is responsible for just twenty pages or 5000-6000 words.

Of course, if you are using content from a virtual summit and 20 presenters, then each chapter becomes only ten pages long. That's enough for an influencer to share their backstory, let them describe their vision going forward, teach a bit about what they do, and provide an example of someone who has achieved a result using their method. If you reduce their page real estate much further, it becomes challenging for them to adequately share their offer, so you risk the book becoming a bit longer. It's your call.

Let's take a slightly different approach because you want to be the sole author this time. You have a 200-page book (double-spaced) with 12 chapters—that's about 16 pages per chapter. Use 2-3 pages for a back-story or context for that module/chapter and 2-3 pages for future-casting and the result they will get when they implement the content.

Now you have ten pages left in that chapter. If each chapter corresponds to a week in your 12-week Mastermind, now you've got two pages per day to teach a skill, assign a task, explain a procedure, invite them to implement a step, plus use some page real estate to provide either one case study/success example per week or one smaller instance per day. You won't have trouble filling the pages, and you will need an editor to reduce your word count and tighten up your delivery. I promise! The fantastic news is that at the end of writing your book… you will have completely created your 12-week Mastermind! Two powerful assets with just one effort, both done in 90 days!

Obviously, you can play around with your book outline to correspond to how many course modules you desire and whatever length of time you choose for your content delivery. There are no rigid rules—but you can see how this improves efficiency for you, letting you do the work once while yielding many different assets. Powerful and strategic!

Meanwhile, savvy and strategic entrepreneurs and small business owners understand that there's a supply chain involved in any industry.

If you are Starbucks, you need a coffee grower and a coffee roaster. You need someone great at real estate and someone who handles insurance, leases, and contracts. You want an HR person. You need someone who does interior design and lighting. You want someone who makes aprons. You need the supplier for all the equipment, and you need the team that cleans the place at night.

Can you see that if you were producing a co-authored book around creating a coffee empire, it would be easy to find topics that didn't compete with you but were complementary, completing the whole picture for the reader? What is your industry's supply chain or ecosystem? Look there for OPE— Other People's Expertise! Likewise, you can employ this same approach to find your "upsells"—your affiliate offers that will complement your offering while bringing value to your clients and exponentially expanding your audience reach. Each person you partner with, either as a co-author or for affiliate offers in your value ladder, has a list and an audience on various platforms. That audience will now know about you at no extra cost because it benefits everyone involved to broadcast the offering authentically.

Perhaps you coach around finance and money management. You wouldn't seek out nine other financial coaches because that would confuse your audience.

Instead, find someone who is an expert in college planning and financial aid options.

Then you might add a marriage counselor or relationship expert who could speak to navigating financial conversations between couples.

You might find an authority in investing for passive income.

You could look for someone who teaches children money management to start them on the right path early.

I'm blue-skying here. Whether your niche falls in health, wealth, or relationships, you can find influencers whose complementary offers will provide value to your audience, as your offer will benefit their audiences. And you only need a handful of other people to participate.

The remarkable thing is I'm not asking you to create your Dream 100 list where you not only have to research and identify 100 people, but somehow you have to approach them and get them to respond to your 'ask.' That's practically an invitation to procrastinate, especially if you don't yet feel like your

Brand recognition or Influence are big enough, yet! That's about to change!

I'm telling you that you can do this with a small handful of other people. If you already have a podcast or summit, you can select content from just ten to twenty people, and you have a co-authored book that is ready to go. Or you can choose just 2-4 influencers with products and services that add value to your customers, and now you don't have to waste time building an offer that is outside your core competency.

You can access my Million Dollar Rolodex here to help you find co-authors, JV or affiliate partners, or folks with skills that will move your business forward fast. **https://www.milliondollarstory.co/mdm-reader-bonus-rolodex**

HOW Do You Accomplish This Result?

Show up....
Just.
Show.
Up!

That's the lesson I learned when I worked in Economic Development.

Once a month, we hosted Board meetings. We had a *huge* Board of Directors composed of all the "movers and shakers" in the city.

We had hospital presidents, university presidents, and bank presidents.

We had the head of the Chamber of Commerce, the head of the Port, and the head of the state power company.

We had owners and CEOs of the biggest companies in town and the COOs of the big hotels.

Elected officials at the city, county, and state-level would come by invitation when the agenda warranted their presence.

Additionally, we always had a few "regular" people attend… every month… as the meetings were open to the public.

I loved that room!

In the center was a gorgeous long, oval table that could seat about 50 people. At one end were massive windows overlooking the river, with blackout shades that opened and closed at the push of a button. The beautiful lighting reflected off the highly polished wood, and the sideboard was filled with delicious food and drink.

The combination of power and tradition meant that people were always impeccably dressed. The distinguished members sat in fabulous chairs in their regular places at the table. In contrast, guests, staff, the public, and the press sat in ordinary chairs lining the room's walls.

Here's what opened my eyes, however.

Folks would start showing up about 30 minutes before beginning every meeting to grab something to eat and have a chance for some quick last-minute conversations before getting down to business. Regardless of title, everyone was on a first-name basis until the actual meeting began. The result was that Howard, the bank president, would greet George, the citizen, with as much warm familiarity as he greeted Rick, the President of the Board. Why? Because he saw George at every meeting and came to perceive him as an equal party to the discussions, even if George had no voting rights.

Because George showed up, becoming someone on a first-name basis with the power-brokers, when sub-committees were formed, or discussions were open, George was selected to participate. Not only did George elevate the status of his voice, but the community benefited from George's perspective, participation, and inclusion.

Tom Shipley is a serial entrepreneur on his way to having

a \$200M/year company. He began hosting a group called the NYC Mastermind to share his business knowledge with local, action-oriented entrepreneurs. Even before COVID, he opened the meeting to zoom attendees, so I joined despite no longer living close to NYC. There I met people with whom I have since done business. And Tom, who regularly hosts notable names in the industry, has been a guest on my podcast. All because I.Showed.Up!

Sometimes it just takes getting in the right room with the right people to help you elevate your authority and business to the next level so you can multiply your income and change not only your world but other people's worlds, too.

Think of a book as a virtual boardroom. Sharing your story widely—through a free lead-magnet, a free+shipping print book, or an audiobook, all leading to your core or high-ticket offers—is like showing up 30 minutes early to greet people who may someday open doors, become friends, or influence your business. As you elevate your brand awareness and visibility, you are now on a first-name basis with power brokers and industry leaders, ready to lift each other up plus make an exponentially more significant impact!

WHO: Carla White! Case Study Success!

Million Dollar Story Author-Entrepreneur Carla White

Let me highlight a member of our Million Dollar Story community. Carla White is a world-renowned author, success coach, and motivational speaker who's spent over a decade helping countless people transform their personal and professional lives. She is the first woman to launch an iPhone app, Gratitude, spending over ten years in the top charts, downloaded by thousands, featured on Oprah, NBC, NYTimes, and countless other publications, and continues to grow in popularity around the globe. She shares everything she knows about producing successful apps in her best seller "Idea to iPhone" (2013). Due to popular demand, she recently launched a podcast aligning neuroscience with ancient wisdom in a way that has never been done before called Radical Shift.

MODULE 3: TURN YOUR SUMMIT OR PODCAST INTO A BOOK

"You are stronger than excuses." Robin Arzón, Peloton

WHAT Result Will You Achieve?

I may be banned from living in the South after saying this. Still, I believe grits are an excuse to eat whatever flavor you choose to mix them with, whether that's brown sugar and melted butter, or shrimp and melted butter, or cheese, which is kind of like melted butter. I know... Bless Her Heart!

Conversely, I grew up in New York City, home of famous *Ray's Pizza*. When I moved away from the city and visited my first Pizza Inn with a team of hungry, undiscerning youngsters after one of my kid's sporting events, I was beyond surprised at the flavors offered. A chain restaurant, it served pizza cafeteria-style and included toppings called 'bacon cheeseburger' or 'loaded baked potato;" I definitely wasn't in the Big Apple anymore. By far, the kids' favorite section was that of the dessert pizzas. Dessert pizza?

Although you may mix and match food ingredients in creative ways that differ by region, you must be more careful mixing platforms for words. Just because you can do something does not mean you should. Only offering up a verbatim transcription of words and calling it a book won't make it palatable, no matter how much butter or sugar you add.

Podcasts—in which a host routinely interviews guests, and summits—filled with expert presenters, are spectacular sources of content on various topics relevant to entrepreneurs. If you choose to create a collaborative work, you are in some ways already ahead of the game because you've accomplished the first step; gathering the influencers.

Beware of merely repurposing content, however. It is critical to tie the subjects together with a curated effort that creates a flowing narrative for the source content. Presumably, your podcast has a theme. For instance, I host *Million Dollar PIVOT*. I consistently ask guests to speak about times they experienced a pivot in business or life and ask them to provide the listeners with tips that helped them navigate their unexpected circumstances.

If I were to create a book from those interviews, I would want to weave one main storyline around them. I might even want to curate the topics so that similar causes were grouped— assembling content around pivots caused by health issues, relationship issues, or external market conditions, for example, for the material to be easier and more logical for the reader to consume.

I might also assemble content around strategies to get past a pivot successfully; in response to a pivot, here's the group that pursued additional education, here's the group that disbanded a partnership and struck out on their own, here's the group that took a break and traveled while they decided what they wanted next, for example. There is more than one way to curate content—just make sure you do!

Likewise, a summit usually gathers speakers with expertise around a core theme: fitness, sales, brands, etc. One might assume that the host provides a framework, a list of questions asked of each presenter. Based on experience or niche, the answers may differ even if, across all speakers, the questions remain the same.

It would genuinely be excruciating and probably confusing to read direct transcripts. Instead, create an outline based on the central result you want your readers to understand due to consuming the information.

This is when you might choose to rely on hybrid ghostwriters and/or a substantive or content editor. These experts will begin with the transcription, use your outline and your core theme, and create structure and flow that make sense. Speakers sometimes head off on tangents and sometimes use many words to describe a situation that a skilled editor can clean up and condense.

It has not been uncommon for the Million Dollar Story Agency teams to start with a transcription of 10,000—15,000 words and conclude with a concise and readable 5500-word chapter. If you haven't tried it yourself, eliminating ten thousand words without losing the voice, tone, or intent of a story requires enormous skill and sensitivity!

WHY Does This Result Matter?

The tagline for this book, *Million Dollar Method^{TM}*, is "Grow Your Influence, Audience, & Revenue Fast." It doesn't say, "How to write a book." Nor does it say, "How to publish a book." It doesn't even say, "How to launch and market a book."

Why?

Let's play a game for a minute. It's called *"What? vs. Who?"*

Which one feels *stronger*? Which one is more *attractive*?

- Award-winning meal
- Award-winning Chef

What about when we attach names? Do you resonate more with the "what" or the "who"?

- Pork schnitzel (his signature dish)
- Wolfgang Puck (product line, restaurant chain, entrepreneur, Chef)

Let's play one more time.

Which one do you recognize or remember IMMEDIATELY? The "what" or the "who"?

- Award-winning play/game
- Award-winning player/team

What about when we attach names?

- The 66th Orange Bowl game. It happened in 2000. Michigan won. It made the record books. Is it coming back to you? No? Not yet?

What about this?

- Tom Brady.

He played in that Orange Bowl game. And "just a few" Super Bowls long after that! But the second you hear his name, you connect with WHO he is. Yes?

I help experts write best-selling books. That's the 'what' and it's the thing so many entrepreneurs say they want to DO. They want to write a book.

I help experts become Best Selling authors.

This transforms YOU, your influence, your brand, your reach, your impact. It is always the "who" who is memorable. You probably can't list the titles of the books Tony Robbins has written but you know WHO he is—and he is a best-selling published author with a strong value-ladder.

The Million Dollar Method^{TM} will indeed result in your having a book. But my promise to you is that you will grow your Influence, your Audience, and your Revenue fast. This is your destination. The book is the vehicle that delivers you there.

You want to write a book. I can help you DO that.

But focus on WHY you want to write a book.

What RESULTS will help your business grow exponentially so you can make the impact you were born to make?

What TRANSFORMATION do you want to take place for you, your brand, your influence so that when people want help, they can easily find you?

We deliver that transformation by making YOU a Best-Selling published author—who just happens to have a Best Selling book—to grow your Influence, your Audience, and your Revenue fast.

The Million Dollar Method^{TM} teaches you how to create a book and your business deliverables simultaneously as a means to an end—the 'end' being growing your influence, audience, and revenue fast. If all I did was teach you how to cook a fabulous meal, but when you were done, you couldn't utilize all those nutrients to stay alive, it would be a completely useless effort.

Million Dollar Story Agency is a publishing and marketing agency. We offer Done-For-You services for either solo-authorship or co-authorship, Done-With-You 12-week Masterminds, and a month-by-month DIY Membership opportunity. All four options help you produce, publish, market and monetize your book. And yet, the book is practically a by-product.

You end up with the very tangible assets of an ebook (for a lead magnet,) a print book (for a free + shipping book funnel,) and an audiobook for a 'bump' offer. Additionally, you have the assets of the marketing funnel and launch promotion to assure Best-Seller status. Further, in addition to everything you need for the low-ticket front-end of your funnel, you also create your core or high-ticket course and funnel. With just one strategy, one effort, you've amplified your brand and your business while producing a book and becoming a published, best-selling author. And you have all this within 90 days, so your business isn't held back waiting for the final result for a year—or more.

From a consumer standpoint, it's useful to produce "a book" across varied formats not only so you can serve up to Amazon the product types they distribute globally, but because different people have different learning styles.

I prefer to hold a physical book, to underline and write notes in the margins. I'm even guilty of dog-earring pages. I also love audiobooks. I spend less time in a car than I used to, but I still consume audio content when I'm exercising, walking the dogs, or doing housework.

Digital books are my least favorite of the three, and if I read a digital book, I do so on a tablet. But my daughter only consumes digital and only on her phone. It's worth serving up all three formats of "a book" to meet your audience where they are most comfortable learning. I do greatly appreciate the live link aspect of ebooks!

From a business strategy, the book (in its varied formats) is simply a tool, an asset, one of many at your disposal. A book is an output produced by becoming a published best-selling author. The Million Dollar Method^{TM} is the multiplier effect, allowing you to produce a book, a funnel, and a complete value ladder to address all aspects of The Profit Pentagon^{TM}.

That ACTION—the act of YOU BECOMING a published best-selling author—is what transitions you from expert to authority. It's what elevates your brand. It's what makes people look at you and think of you differently—and think of you when they are problem-aware and seeking a solution. It's what elevates your status. It's what opens new doors, gets you invited to more prominent podcasts, bigger stages, and more significant PR opportunities. It's what moves you closer to receiving your verified Blue Checkmark on IG and FB so that you keep reaching a broader distribution, which you can then monetize, so you are continually diversifying your passive income sources.

And those attributes combined are what let you make a more significant impact, a bigger difference, effect more change and create a movement if you want to do so.

When you co-author a book or join a mastermind or membership program, the book is still the output. Still, the additional ACTION that happens is that of relationship building. I have spent tens of thousands of dollars joining masterminds. The PRIMARY significance of those, the ONE thing that has advanced my business more than any skill or tool I acquired, is relationship building.

Identifying and collaborating with like-minded mission-and-success-driven influencers—people who have become friends, people for whom I have enormous respect and admiration, people who lead by example—has been the single most significant game-changer for my business. It's only growing from here as more and more people join the Million Dollar Story community.

Your podcast episodes, summits, co-authored books, blogs, YouTube content, Facebook lives, or media articles will yield the same fruit when you strategically approach them, knowing why you want to write a book. It's genuinely not so you can have printed pages of transcribed words that you assemble into a paperweight.

HOW Do You Accomplish This Result?

You've probably heard variations of this over the years:

Good + Fast = Expensive
Good + Cheap = Slow
Fast + Cheap = Garbage

The same thing comes into play with editing—and I'm not talking about proofing for misspelling or extra spaces between words because there is free or inexpensive software for that.

I'm speaking about a trained professional human who reads and considers the work as a whole and addresses the content flow of source text as mentioned above. You pay based on their experience, how much work the content requires, and in what time frame you want the project returned. (Make sure to negotiate for at least one revision.) It should go without saying, but you will pay dearly if you want a turnaround time of fewer than six months.

Editors charge differently depending on the genre and for fiction vs. non-fiction. When an editor is doing what I refer to as hybrid ghostwriting, they charge based on their need to maintain the writer's voice, tone, and aesthetics while intensely editing the content for comprehension, consistency, and flow—not just across the chapter or section, but with an eye towards the entire body of work.

This is especially challenging when you are assembling an anthology of many different voices, content delivery approaches, and speaking styles. Some summit presenters or podcast interviewees are very logical and speak to bullet points. Others lean more towards rambling stories. The "ghostwriting" editor is faced with an enormous task to produce something palatable and logical for the reader while assuring the audiences will still recognize their experts.

The task to edit the work of a sole voice might be easier from a consistency standpoint, but if the author rambles, is redundant, or references too much tech-speak, an editor's role is still challenging—and crucial.

Googling price per word will yield a variety of rates. Know that what looks cheap may produce unacceptable results because it will have been software, not an experienced, trained human who does the heavy lifting. That alone can lose the voice of the speaker. You also want to look for a native English speaker—especially if English is not the first language of the author- entrepreneur, and the primary audience will be English speakers.

The *average* for business non-fiction for content or developmental editing is $0.0315 per word... so for a book that's roughly 60K words (about 200 pages) in length, that first layer of editing alone will cost $1890. Add $$ if you want the work returned in less than six months. Keep in mind, a good editor is in high demand, and your project is not the only one on their calendar.

Now add copy-editing—for business non-fiction—at an average of $0.022 per word. That's another $1320. Cap that off with proofreading at $0.0125 per word, and you've tacked on another $750. While you may be tempted to skimp here, we have all experienced reading books with a noticeable number of "oops, they missed that" sensations. Indeed, if it's written by someone you admire, it's hard to ignore. One or two 'oops' per book is expected and forgivable because we aren't perfect—but more than that makes me squirm in discomfort; I expect more from a leading expert, don't you?

Your grand total to go from transcription to finished product, on average, only for editing? Just under $4000!

Can you outsource this for less? Of course—just as you could outsource it for more. Refer back to the recipe for good, fast, cheap, quality, or junk outcome! Can you do this in-house, or even yourself? Yes—just know that it's an opportunity cost. When you or your team devote time and treasure to this effort, some other thing is delayed.

Also, let me offer food for thought... Creating a book from transcripts of podcasts and summit interviews is a project. That implies you need a project manager—which often is you. Can you fit this into your regular to-do list for organizing a summit or running a podcast show?

Once the editing is done, you must have the opportunity for a final review and an opportunity for a second light revision. Suppose we're discussing an anthology comprised of podcast guests or summit presenters or simply a co-authored effort. In that case, each content author must have the chance, before publishing, to review for accuracy—names, dates, stories—to ensure that nothing published with their name attached is a misrepresentation of what they said.

Additionally, much like any hire, hiring an editor or editing team requires interviewing and determining who possesses the skills they state they have. Further, do they communicate well, do they respect your requirements, do they respond in a timely fashion, and deliver on time and budget? Do they understand your vision, and are they aligned with your values and the community you serve? Are they receptive to your feedback and requests?

If not, it's back to the drawing board. It's not only your name and reputation on this project—it's the name and reputation of every influencer whose content you are repurposing. Of course, you want the finished product to appropriately reflect great value and quality. That won't necessarily happen without your precious resources of time, effort, and attention.

Small rant warning: I have heard big names in the coaching industry and other non-publishing industries imply that writing a book is easy. They say, "Walk and talk." They then instruct you to find someone on Fivver who is "not in it for the money" to take your transcription and create a best-selling book from it. Yep, that usually makes my blood pressure rise like a rocket launch!

As coaches or consultants, they charge $500-$2000 or more per hour, perhaps paid monthly, for their expertise. If they deliver value and that value helps you make progress, go for it. They charge what the market will bear and what their results have earned them, as does any entrepreneur.

Yet they are demeaning another expert by implying that if they charge more than $10-$15/hour or a few hundred dollars per project, they must be "in it for the money." For shame!

Don't be the person who does not recognize and reward the expertise of the various types of editors. And remember, there is one price point for average delivery time and a higher price point for rushed delivery, or moving your project to the front of the line ahead of other already-scheduled work. Good editing, the cornerstone to the quality of your entire project, is NOT a commodity to be purchased based on the lowest price. You will get what you pay for! End small rant! :)

Where do you find editors?

Ask within your community. Or turn to any of the following:

- Fiverr
- Upwork
- Reedsy

- Manuscript Wishlist
- Million Dollar Story Agency

Also, know there are no less than a bajillion boutique publishers and small imprints who will promise to take on your whole project from draft manuscript to final publishing of your ebook. Some will also include a print book. Fewer still will offer an audiobook for around $6000. And a handful will also provide marketing for an additional $20k-$50k. There is *not* a shortage of services or fulfillment companies.

Revisit your goals, your mission, and your vision.

Why are you considering authoring or producing a book?

Where does it fit into your business strategy?

Is the book the endgame?

If so, any of these service offerings can do fulfillment; you can check the box and move on. How anticlimactic!

After editing, comes wrapping the book up in its package—cover graphics, ISBN and barcode, interior layout & design, etc.

If you have an in-house designer or enjoy graphic design, you can make a reasonably decent cover yourself. Decide if you want the cover to be matte or glossy. Typically, a non-fiction book has a glossy cover. The file format should be TIFF or JPEG, and the cover image size for an ebook should be a minimum of 625 pixels wide and 1000 pixels long, while the best quality is 2,560 x 1,600 pixels.

To create a cover for a print book, you first must know the book's page count AFTER the final layout & design is complete. You must determine the size of the book (usually 6 X 9), the color of the paper (white or cream), and the color of the interior (B&W or color.) The graphic designer uses this information to correctly determine the spine's exact width to fit your print book (referred to as a trade paperback) correctly.

Also, recall that I urge you to have the first two pages of your book plus the last two pages of your book be a place for ads and a CTA to leave a review for your book. A graphic designer can help with these four pages as well.

Here are more options for help with graphic design.

- Canva
- Adobe Photoshop
- Fiverr
- Upwork
- 99Designs

- AuthorLab
- Unsplash
- Million Dollar Story Agency

CreateSpace has migrated into KDP, Kindle Direct Publishing. BookBaby and Lulu are predominantly geared towards book printing. Know that each of these services caters to authors desiring to self-publish in ALL categories, including fiction; many tools on these sites have zilch to do with entrepreneurship and business.

If you are determined to self-publish, here's a brief video with some how-to pointers for you. **https://www.milliondollarstory.co/self-publish-mdm-reader-bonus**

Be sure to have the following in place when your book is formatted:

1. Title page
2. Copyright page
3. Free Offer pointing to an optin page to collect email address (two pages)
4. Table of Contents
5. A Dedication Page if you want one
6. Advance Praise/Endorsements
7. The Body (Your actual book content)

a. Preface (non-fiction)

b. Introduction

c. Chapters/Sections—Speakers/Presenters/
   Course Modules

8. Back matter

   a. Epilogue

   b. Author Headshot(s)

   c. Author Bio(s)

   d. References, if applicable

   e. Free Offer pointing to an optin page to
      collect email address (one page)

   f. CTA—request reader to leave a review

From here, follow all the same guidelines noted in Chapters 4 and 6.

Kdp.amazon.com will walk you through the entire self-publishing process for free, and if you only publish an ebook, you don't even need to purchase an ISBN.

When it's time to publish, select your keyword strings and your categories. Make sure you did your research so that your title, subtitle, and keyword strings are SEO'd/SEM'd. Get copy help for your book description and back cover copy. Select two categories and then contact support to upgrade that to ten US categories—and ten categories per additional non-US market you choose to enter.

Help your presenters/speakers/authors create their author pages and link them to the book once it is live on Amazon. If you want to know how you and your authors can easily create author pages, grab my 'How To' guide here. **https://www.milliondollarstory.co/author-page-creation-mdm-reader-bonus**

Select your book price. Choose your launch day/date/time and organize your authors' free offers to help promote the launch.

Run your Amazon ads and FB ads. Write and distribute your press releases. Work to get verified Amazon reviews—20 at a bare minimum.

A book is a powerful marketing tool, which is why all the big names have them—Russell Brunson, Dean Graziosi, Gary Vaynerchuk, Dan Kennedy, Tony Robbins, Brendon Burchard, and many, many more.

Suppose you are organizing content from your summit or podcast into a book. In that case, you are offering a highly valuable tool for your colleagues. You will either spend a great deal of time and sweat equity or some significant outlay of cash or both to produce a high-quality book from the original transcripts.

How do you not eat those costs yourself?

For this example, we will use whole numbers.

Let's decide your summit has 30 speakers, or you have chosen 30 episodes from your podcast in which you have interviewed experts. You will feature just 16 of those in your "free offer" marketing funnel on launch day, giving extra publicity to those 16 entrepreneurs and creating an additional evergreen lead source for each of them.

To participate as one of those 16 featured, the marketing cost is a very reasonable $1000 per participant. One way to approach who gets featured in these 16 spots is to look at market reach. Ideally, each of these 16 will have a combined audience size (email list, LI, FB, IG, Clubhouse, or other social media platform following) of *at least 5000*. That translates into an existing distribution reach of 80,000 sets of eyeballs with no ad spend.

You have an additional 14 author-entrepreneurs who also have content in your book (16 + 14 = 30 summit presenters.) You choose whether to charge them $500 or $250 each. That will translate into either $7000 or $3500. Let's say you go with the higher number. Between the "pay to play" marketing fee of having your lead magnet featured in the launch marketing funnel or the smaller "pay to play" marketing fee of being featured in a soon-to-be best selling published book, across the 30 participants, you have now offset your out-of-pocket costs by $23,000.

Not that it's my job to convince you of your worth, but let's examine this from a different angle. Let's pretend you suddenly became an expert in book editing, publishing, and marketing. Instead of outsourcing some or all of this project, you chose to do 100% of it yourself. Let's keep this fantasy going. You had zero learning curve, and you only invested two hours a day of your time for twelve weeks. We all know that doing every aspect of this job, not the least of which is project management and communication with 30 people, likely took more time than that. Still, since we're in pretend mode, we will let you accomplish miracles.

Your miraculous self valued your time at less than $200/hour!

Meanwhile, you incurred the opportunity cost of 120 hours of lost time and focus from your core business over those same three months.

All of which is to say, collecting $23,000 from your podcast guests or summit presenters to be featured in a published bestselling book is a sweet deal for them and, in truth, allows you to break even but not much more.

I agree that you could download the transcripts, assemble them into a doc, throw a jpg on top, upload it on Amazon, and call it a book.

Please never tell me if that's what you do!

Please don't be that person who devalues yourself, your speakers, your content, your vendors, and your audience looking for help in such a way that you don't exert real effort into creating a quality product that will endure and serve at the highest level.

For those of you who anticipate you will want to create a book from an upcoming summit, be sure to include terms around who owns the content. It's likely to be similar to the contract they sign to participate in your summit but clear the language in advance with your attorney to be safe.

Have the conversation about the opportunity to participate in the book when you invite them to the summit or podcast. It will be more streamlined for your planning to know who's in, plus collect payment, in advance.

There are likely to be summit presenters of whom you make zero asks just because of who they are. If you invite a massive influencer as an anchor for your summit, a means to attract other presenters, sometimes merely having them show up is more than enough. You don't expect them to promote your summit, pay to participate, or even join in affiliate offers. It's more than enough only for these 'big fish' to show up.

Ask them to be in your book anyway. These influencers often understand it's a time for them to contribute to both the visibility of rising entrepreneurs and their collective audiences. They are service and impact-driven, and this is a chance for them to give back. So ask! The value of their brand authority (the very thing you aim for by choosing the strategy of becoming a best-selling author) attached to your project can be considered in-kind payment. No money changes hands.

WHO: Evans Putman! Case Study Success!

Million Dollar Story Author-Entrepreneur Evans Putman

Let me highlight a member of our Million Dollar Story community. Evans is a coach and consultant who helps purpose-driven entrepreneurs and changemakers create profitable, scalable dream client businesses that align with their core values, serve their ideal customers, and turn their missions into movements. He has over 20 years of experience building successful businesses as an online entrepreneur, and his training has been featured in ClickFunnels Founder Russell Brunson's high-ticket coaching program. Evans' 7-Figure Podcast Blueprint gives coaches, consultants, course creators, and other expert entrepreneurs a proven system to turn a podcast into an automated traffic, leads, and high-ticket sales machine. He is also the host of the Infinite Impact Influencers podcast and creator of the Infinite Impact Method™. Learn more and get your blueprint to increase income, ignite impact, and transform lives at *www.EvansPutman.com*

LEAD CONVERSION & SALES

MODULE 4: WRITE, PUBLISH, MARKET, & MONETIZE

"We are dreamers who hustle." Robin Arzón, Peloton

WHAT Result Will You Achieve?

- Backstory: WHAT—How I learned/earned what I'm about to give you
- Strategy: WHY—this goal & it's steps are relevant/ key >> RESULT
- Tactics: HOW—Step by Step How-To (direct them to a course for more HOW)
- Case Study: WHO—give examples of success >> Result they can picture having)

When Million Dollar Story Agency produced the book *Million Dollar Dads*, it took just 50 days from when I had a sales call with one of the authors to the time he was a published best-selling author. His authority is firmly established as he is now a Best Seller in nine categories relevant to his work. But, perhaps more importantly, with zero extra time or effort on his part, he expanded his audience reach by tens of thousands in less than two months!

Let me say this differently. He wrote a best-selling book and became a published best-selling author *while* parenting five children, running his company, fulfilling large contracts, volunteering, being on various town boards, and doing 75Hard!

Recently I spoke with a colleague, someone I've known for decades, about ghostwriting. He'd had the opportunity to work on projects with publishing companies that deliver Wall Street Journal and NYTimes Best Sellers for their authors. Traditionally these publishing houses, even the small ones, take one to two years to produce and market a book. However, I hadn't realized that it's not uncommon for some of these firms to charge in the millions! As in—for the busy executive of a large global corporation who wants a book ghostwritten and then extensively marketed—the fee ranges from upwards of three million dollars!

Contrast that with self-publishing a book, which can be done for a mere few hundred dollars. Why is someone willing to pay $2 million or $3 million or more to publish a book when technically it can be accomplished for a few hundred dollars?

I return to the question I ask prospective clients; "What has to happen to consider the result that you get a success?" Which is simply another way of saying, "Why do you want to write a book? What will the book DO for you and your business?"

Listen to what Peng Joon and Dan Henry say about choosing to become a published author to position your brand authority—you can access the video here:

https://www.milliondollarstory.co/brand-authority-advice-mdm-reader-bonus

WHY Does This Result Matter?

The Million Dollar Method^{TM} focuses on the following Blue Ocean methodology we refer to as SEAS:

Speed
Ease

Assets

Status

The Million Dollar Method^{TM} is designed to yield the following RESULTS:

Speed—to market; you will be a published Amazon best-selling author in 90 days or less. You will ALSO have, if you choose, a complete value ladder of offers for your business.

Ease—you don't have to write, and you don't have to do any extra advance marketing.

Assets—ebook, print book, audiobook, marketing funnel, evergreen lead gen, and all facets of The Profit Pentagon^{TM}.

Status—you transition from Expert to Authority, you build your Brand, you elevate your visibility, you network with influencers in the Million Dollar Story community; you are both a PUBLISHED author and a BEST SELLING author with a warm intro to numerous audiences while being part of an exclusive 'inner circle' of published best-selling authors.

You can look for an entity that will help you WRITE—or you can take it upon yourself to figure the writing portion out.

Nod your head when you identify as 'some people' below. Say, "That's ME!"

- Some people don't like to write or aren't confident in their writing.
- Some people don't have time to write.
- Some people can't decide what to write about, so getting started is a challenge.
- Some people struggle to finish in a time frame such that their content is still relevant either to their own business or the larger market.
- Some people think writing a book now or this year isn't a priority.
- Some people think that since they wrote one book, they can stop there.
- Some people think that when they write a book, it will not be with co-authors.
- Some people think, if they have one Best Seller, there is no point in doing it again.

I'm thinking out loud here, but do Olympic athletes retire after winning just one event? Did Jack Canfield, responsible for a series that has sold over a half-Billion copies (yes, with a "b,") proclaim one book was enough? The majority of books Canfield has written have been co-authored. Last thought— name an Influencer (Tony Robbins, Brendon Burchard, Dean Graziosi, Russell Brunson, and more) who only has one book.

Do you suppose they are a tad busy running their multi-million dollar companies?

Points taken.

The next step is to PUBLISH.

You can undoubtedly follow directions to do this yourself.

You want an ebook as a free or low-price lead magnet, a print book for your 'free + shipping' book funnel, and an audiobook for your 'bump' offer. We will cover the actual steps to produce these three formats a little bit later.

Next, you want an OTO—a one-time offer—as your core offer or premium offer. And then, ideally, you have some "upsells" and "downsells." When you write strategically, you also produce a course or Mastermind. Then, you can create a funnel that delivers it or create a funnel where prospects get on your calendar for a sales call. Good thing your book has done the work for you of establishing a relationship with your prospect, so they already know, like, and trust you and your results.

In a co-published work, consider not only your professional reputation but that of your colleagues and fellow influencers. It should go without saying you want your book to be professionally produced so that when it appears next to books with substantial budgets, yours won't be dismissed.

Now you've produced your content and published your content. The following steps are to market your book so that you monetize it.... Produce. Publish. Market. Monetize. Those are your marching orders. And we want you to do that speedily and easily, resulting in assets and authority.

HOW Do You Accomplish This Result?

It's so evident that it's easy to skip it; what is the *title* of your book going to be?

Naming your book feels personal and may be tied to your brand or a theme, but keep it short just as other Best Selling books in business and entrepreneurship have done.

If you ask others to join you in co-authoring around a theme, having a working title in mind will help bring them on board as it did in my "Dads" and "Moms" books.

Here are some examples of short titles of highly influential books:

- *"Start With Why"*

- *"Who Not How"*
- *"The Miracle Morning"*
- *"Good To Great"*
- *"Million Dollar Dads"*
- *"Million Dollar Method^{TM}"*

The subtitle is more critical than the title from a ranking perspective and can be longer than three words. I recommend crafting the subtitle after the content is complete. Your subtitle should not only illuminate what the book is about, but it should also target keywords and be optimized for search engines. In other words, do your SEO research when you create your subtitle.

Speed is essential for a busy, influential entrepreneur. We are implementers. We take action. We know what problems and pain points our audience has. We want solutions for them now. Importantly, we are here to make a difference and serve our customers. That can't happen if the process of becoming a published, best-selling author takes too long.

The Million Dollar Method^{TM} uses a Trello board, linked Google folders, and some new software for organization.

If the result you desire is to produce your own book and value ladder, our first step is to be clear regarding the results you get for your clients. Knowing where you're taking them and what steps are needed along the way will let you create your course modules and your book outline.

If you choose to produce a collaborative work, determine what influencers will contribute to the content. You can join with other entrepreneurs around a theme in health, wealth, or relationships.

As just discussed in Module 3, if you host a podcast, you may choose to repurpose content from guests you have interviewed. Likewise, if you host a virtual summit, you may decide to repurpose content from presenters.

As already mentioned, but it's vital, be sure to refer back to agreements you have made with your guests and presenters regarding how you may use the content and copyright to the material.

When you partner with other influencers to create brand new content, or as you convert prospects into customers, you can use DocuSign, SignNow, or some other contract software that lets others sign agreements with electronic signatures.

It's common for high-level influencers to have assistants. While obvious, don't overlook collecting contact information for both the author-entrepreneur and their assistant: name, email, mobile if you will be contacting them via text and their name on Voxer or WhatsApp. Additionally, be sure to get their "snail mail" address so you can mail them physical copies of the book or any gift once the paperback is published.

Million Dollar Story Agency gifts its authors copies of the book once the cover is updated to reflect best-seller status. Our entrepreneurs and their families are always delighted to receive them!

Suppose you are using content initially recorded for a podcast or summit. In that case, you can organize it around the questions you have already asked.

If you are beginning from scratch, decide on four to five central topics or questions to address in each chapter/course module or ask each co-contributor. While their answers will reflect different experiences, continuity throughout the book will be maintained based on topics and your framework.

For instance, in this book, you will observe that the Million Dollar Method^{TM} uses the framework of What (Result), Why (Future-Casting), How (Systems & Processes), and Who (Case Study) for each of our chapters. They correspond to course modules in our Mastermind course and our Membership program. The Profit Pentagon^{TM} is the "what"—or the result—the book delivers, and The Million Dollar Method^{TM} is the "how" it is delivered.

Once you know your course and book outline and have determined your framework or set of questions, record your responses to the question set. Refer to the Trello board for instructions as well as deadlines! Save your recordings as an mp3 or m4a in a google folder. I use Voice Memo on my iPhone and simply share the m4a file. It couldn't be easier. If you are the only author using our Done-For-You services, we take it from here. If you are running a collaborative project, direct your co-authors to the shared folder for recorded files.

My author-entrepreneurs with young children often use the time before anyone wakes up or after they've gone to sleep to record. Or they take the dog for a walk and record while walking! Some author-entrepreneurs sit in their cars—but I recommend being in a parked car! I love to sit downtown by the water to record.

If you want a copy of the Million Dollar Method^{TM} Trello board, you can grab that here: **https://www.milliondollarstory.co/trello-board-template-mdm-reader-bonus**

If you have the expertise and see the merit in becoming a published, best-selling co-author in an upcoming Million Dollar Story, be sure to get on our waiting list here. **https://www.milliondollarstory.co/write-that-book-this-year**

Obtaining endorsements, or Advance Praise, is another tool for increasing the distribution of your book. An advantage to co-authoring is that you can tap into a collective extended network. Reach high. Suppose each entrepreneur extends an invitation to one-to-three of their most important contacts.

In that case, the book is likely to have at least a few strong endorsements. The disadvantage is that sometimes the contact chooses to endorse the individual and not the book itself. If you find yourself seeking endorsements for a collaborative work, be quite clear about what will be helpful and what won't work for the team.

When asking for endorsements, it's best to write a short sample paragraph and send it along with a chapter, if not the whole book, in draft form. But because our process moves so fast, before anything is even written, contact your potential reviewers and put them on notice. Let them know that you'd love to have their participation. Note that you will provide suggested verbiage that they may amend and invite them to provide their name, their title, and their URL. Be sure to ask them for their mailing address so you may send them a physical copy and alert them to the launch date to let their audience know of the value available to them with the book's release.

The endorsements will need a quick review and copy edit before being added into the final draft and before it's sent to interior formatting, also known as 'layout and design'—which has to be done for both an ebook and a print book.

Let's back up to a high-level view of the Million Dollar Method^{TM} for a minute. Your goal is to have a thriving business with a constant inflow of warm prospects who feel nurtured, buy quickly and often, join your movement, thus elevating your influence, audience reach, and revenue. You want one method that strategically delivers all of that with the least amount of your resources of time, money, effort, and opportunity cost.

You decide it's a smart strategy to be a published best-selling author, transforming yourself from an expert to an Authority with a solid brand to attract highly qualified clients.

You share your stories, inspire belief in the future via your solutions, teach, and demonstrate potential for success through case studies to nurture your readers and prospects. As they come to know you through your storytelling, they build a relationship with you.

With each successive chapter, you meet and dismiss objections. You evoke emotions, acknowledging their pain, and clearly describe the path to alleviate those barriers quickly. By the time you have a call to action, your conversion time and costs have gone down because

they are now a warm lead who trusts you and your offer.

You create multiple assets for your value ladder, grow your list exponentially, and charge premium prices while having an evergreen lead gen source. With one strategic 90-day effort, you create your front-end and your core or premium offers—and your book!

Finally, you have built your brand, elevated your visibility, and established your authority with minimal stress, time, effort, or ad spend! As a result, you find yourself invited to more influential podcasts, summits, media, affiliate, and speaking opportunities. The snowball effect grows as your brand awareness attracts increasingly more attention, making it easier to retain and ascend your current customers.

You have written a best-selling book, become a published best-selling author & you have grown your influence, audience, and revenue fast!

I love to write, and I feel confident in my writing skills, but I find it challenging to carve out time without interruptions. But finding 15 minutes here and there to record is easy!

Once you, or you and your co-authors, have recorded the content—or if you are working with podcast or summit content—the next step is editing.

Think of it like heading in to get your hair done. Depending on the state of your hair, you may need a quick trim (proofreading,) or you may need a wash and blowdry before your haircut, which will take a bit more time and attention (copy editing,) or you may be headed in for deep conditioning, color treatment, and styling (content editing) to walk out as a 'new you!'

The spoken word is quite different from text. Suppose you simply fill pages with direct transcripts. The value of the messaging will be entirely lost as it will be so excruciating to read. Additionally, each speaker has a different voice; you don't want to lose their voice, but you must have continuity across chapters within the book.

You may have heard Dean Graziosi's story about writing his first book and being rejected by his editor because his grammar and sentence structure were quite conversational and directed to his readers. That criticism and rejection sent him into a depression with a heavy dose of imposter syndrome;

who was he to write a book? But, of course, he went on to write and sell many widely distributed and incredibly successful books because he found a different editor and publisher who embraced his voice and style!

In our Done-For-You offers, Million Dollar Story Agency uses ghostwriters in a hybrid sense. They take the transcriptions from your recordings as their base starting point but transform the content into a more logical, readable flow while maintaining a significant degree of the original speaker's voice—just as Dean's new publisher did for him. Next, we use a team of content editors, then progress to the final step of proofreading. It is super helpful to have different teams for these different stages. The Million Dollar Method^{TM} shows you how to do the same for your content.

Of course, we aren't aiming for the quality of literary fiction nor the complexity of scientific or academic writing. We don't want to take away anyone's voice. Still, we do want a finished product that reflects the professional status of the author-entrepreneurs.

It is worth noting that if you produce a collaborative effort targeting multiple audiences, you will want to agree in advance on some basics around content and language. Is it OK to include religious or political views? Is it OK to use the F-bomb? Gary Vaynerchuk and Garrett J White love the F-bomb, and their audiences love them. There is no right or wrong answer here—you just need to consider it before you have an unexpected controversy on your hands. Even when you control 100% of the content, consider the ideal audience you want to attract. Some language or topics may be more or less polarizing depending on your targeted prospect's age and geographic location.

The strategy behind writing a non-fiction business-centric book is to quickly and easily create an evergreen source of leads for a widely expanded audience and move them to your value ladder, which you create simultaneously using The Million Dollar Method^{TM}. Remember the business pillars of The Profit Pentagon^{TM}: Lead Generation & Prospecting, Lead Nurture & Relationship building, Lead Conversion & Sales, Client Delivery & Fulfillment, Client Retention & Ascension. Writing the right book incorporates all of these.

In your work—whether it's the whole book or just one chapter—as you speak to your new prospects, you nurture them, let them see who you are and how you show up in the world. You can be vulnerable, demonstrating that you understand their pain because you have been where they are now. The sales conversation is now stress-free and straightforward because, having read your chapter, they have become raving fans. They already know they want to work with you. All that's left is for you to deliver the thing you're the expert in. Because you strategically wrote a book while simultaneously creating your offers, delivery is easy. You send them to your value ladder with the intent to grow their experience to achieve their desire so that you can retain those clients for lifetime value.

If you want a jumpstart in the strategy behind using a book in your value ladder, be sure to download a free copy of my Publishing Profit Guide here **https://www.milliondollarstory.co/publishing-guide**

Let's keep going.

You've written, so now you're ready to publish.

Remember the good news! You do not need to write a query letter or a book proposal.

You do not need to secure a literary agent or be rejected by publishers.

Million Dollar Story Agency has its imprint (a fancy way of saying we have our in-house publisher), or you can choose the self-publishing route.

Dan Henry will tell you that he went with a small imprint, also known as a boutique publisher because that route avoids the disadvantages of both self-publishing and pursuing big publishing houses.

An ebook and a print book have different formatting requirements. Here are the steps you have checked off so far—you have:

- Completed all levels of editing
- Gotten your cover designed
- Determined the copyright through contracts of who owns what content (if there are multiple authors; otherwise, simply negotiate with your publisher for ownership of your copy)
- Assembled your Table of Contents
- Collected endorsements
- Written your acknowledgments, the Preface, and the Epilogue
- Included bios and headshots for your co-authors, or simply updated your own
- Checked to be sure all URLs and links within the text work (please triple check this one!)

Now it's time for interior formatting—otherwise known as layout and design.

EPUB is the standard ebook format that everybody except Amazon uses; they use MOBI for Kindle.

If you self-publish your ebook on Amazon KDP, you can use EPUB, MOBI, an HTML file, or even a doc or Docx file.

If you are determined to self-publish, here's a brief video with some how-to pointers for you: **https://www.milliondollarstory.co/self-publish-mdm-reader-bonus**

There are two kinds of EPUB. Since our books are text-heavy, we use standard, reflowable EPUB rather than the fixed-layout EPUB. If you include images, you'll need to optimize them and place them inline as the text cannot flow around images.

Consider using standard fonts like Georgia or Times New Roman for your body text and a sans serif font like Arial or Helvetica for your headings. Scrivener is a tool for iOS and Windows that lets you export your book to EPUB format automatically. Finally, Vellum Press is a formatting tool for print and digital formatting.

For a print book, a PDF is all that you need.

As a refresher, your format options are digital, audio, hard-cover, and paperback.

In the industry, the term used is 'trade paperback'—you choose the size, which will range anywhere from 5.5" x 8.5" (a size that's called digest) to 6" x 9" (also known as US trade.) This is the go-to paperback size range for many novels, memoirs, and non-fiction books in today's market.

You must specify the size for your graphic designer as well as the color of the paper (white or cream,) whether you want your cover to be glossy or matte, if the interior will include color or be only black & white, and the final page count, for the graphic designer to create one image PDF where the spine will be the correct width for your book.

There is some crucial real estate inside your book that I don't want you to overlook.

Take any paperback book off your bookshelf. First, you see the outside cover, and then you open to the inside cover. The next page is the title page and includes your copyright information, the name of your publisher, editor, designer, etc. Most people move straight to the Table of Contents, but that is a terrible waste of an opportunity!

The first two and last two pages are prime real estate! It's like a magazine where the most expensive ad space is the inside front cover and the back cover because everyone sees those, right?

BONUS MATERIALS!

If you're ready to become a published, bestselling author fast, even if you don't like to write or don't have time, we have solutions! Ask to JOIN our FREE group, schedule a FREE CALL and download our FREE book:

Mastermind Community:
https://app.socialfunnels.io/access/influencercircle

Become A Published Author Without Writing A Word:
https://milliondollarstory.co

I'd also like to give you a free copy my bestselling ebook,
Million Dollar Story, Vol 1
https://milliondollarstory.co/ebook-Vol1

On Amazon, the 'Look Inside' feature shows people content at the beginning of the book. It is effectively another free lead-gen source for you! Use your front two pages to offer free bonuses. Send readers to an opt-in page where you provide a free lead magnet in exchange for getting their email address. Each chapter will also teach, give value, and direct readers to resources. But don't wait! A collective audience—of tens of thousands of people—is potentially going to read the book. Let them know immediately that you are ready to serve them and make a difference for them!

BIG FAVOR TO ASK–WILL YOU HELP?

Thank You For Reading *Million Dollar Dads*!

I really appreciate your feedback, and I love hearing your ideas about the book and how you relate to these stories. The authors and team at Million Dollar Story Agency want to know that the stories they tell and we produce are making a difference!

Please go to Amazon today and share your thoughts about the book. We appreciate your time and feedback ginormously!

Thanks again!
~ Jamie Wolf

On the very last interior page, have a CTA—a call to action. Ask your readers to leave a review. One thing that adds to whether your book will attain bestseller status and stay in the top 100 is the number of verified reviews your book has. We're making the assumption you have produced an excellent book that will garner favorable reviews! Show people how to go to Amazon, rate the book, leave a review, and offer them a thank you in exchange for taking that action.

Don't overlook the precious real estate that you've got in your book.

If you aren't ready to purchase and learn how to use formatting software, you can look for someone who does graphic design for the print covers and someone who does interior formatting. Sources of freelancers include Fiverr, Upwork, Reedsy, and PubLaunch. Million Dollar Story Agency can also provide Layout & Design for your ebook and print book. Be sure to pay for the level that lets you keep the source files. If you want 3D mockups to work with for marketing, you can buy those from freelancers or use AuthorLab.

The global audiobooks market size was close to $3Billion USD in 2019 (with books at $145B USD) and is expected to expand at a compound annual growth rate (CAGR) of close to 25% in the next several years. (Deloitte) So you will also want to be sure to take your final content and produce an audiobook that meets ACX guidelines.

JAMIE WOLF

You can either read your own work (or in an anthology project have your authors read their final edited chapters,) or you can hire a narrator. Once your audio editor has produced all the necessary files, Amazon takes a minimum of 30 days to review and approve your audiobook. Any rejection starts the 30-day count all over again, so see if you can find someone who gets it right the first time!

It's best to provide your authors with instructions on narration. Even if you and they routinely record for podcasts, controlling sound and background noise to assure your audio editor won't have to spend hundreds of hours editing is crucial. Remember, a 200-page book produces roughly six hours of recorded content. That is potentially a LOT of editing.

Feel free to pick up a copy of the Narration Guide I give my authors here.

https://www.milliondollarstory.co/audiobook-narration-guide-mdm-reader-bonus

Let's recap the publishing portion....

- You have a title.
- You have a subtitle optimized for SEO.
- You have professionally designed graphics for the front cover.

116

- You have completed the process of creating—or repurposing—content and having it edited professionally.
- You have a professionally formatted interior.
- If you publish only an ebook on Kindle, you do not need an ISBN.
- If you self-publish a paperback book on Amazon, they will provide an ISBN for you.

If you want to know more about when to use an ISBN or a Library of Congress number or how to acquire either, you can watch a short video here. **https://www.milliondollarstory.co/isbn-how-and-when-to-use-one-mdm-reader-bonus**

What's left as far as publishing your book? Glad you asked!

Three things are left, which all matter when it comes to how—or if—your book will rank well on Amazon. Remember that more than two million new titles are published every year, so you don't want to waste opportunities to stand out. Your job is to make sure people are aware of your book amidst the noise, so they have the chance to benefit from its content!

The first is the back cover "copy" of your paperback or hardcover book, which is also your book's description on the Amazon sales page (which is also sometimes referred to as a "book blurb.")

Look at most back covers. You will see the book's title, a bar code of the ISBN, the publishing company's name if it's not a self-published work, and sometimes a picture of the author if there is only one.

But the real value comes from the copy that both describes your book using keywords and entices readers with what promises to be content they don't want to miss. So, for example, if you have an excerpt from an endorsement from a well-known authority, you can, and should, include that on the back cover if you have not already put it on the front cover.

For those of you who have heard of "copy" or copywriting before, you know that you want excellent copy for your sales funnels, ads, emails, even your posts—any place you touch a prospect. It's no different here. Your copy needs to be well-written, and it needs to help your book rank on Amazon.

Here's a cool tip: once you have your back cover copy written, you can use at least some of it in your press releases and Amazon ads to make them stand out more!

Second, when you upload your ebook or any other format of your book, you have the opportunity to include up to seven keyword strings. The keyword strings are limited to 50 characters. They should be relevant to the book's content and the strongest trending or searched terms when the book launches. They should not repeat anything in the subtitle.

The third remaining item to attend to is choosing categories, sub-categories, and occasionally sub-sub-categories. Regarding categories, be aware that they are slightly different for ebooks than for 'books'—and they also change by country.

Region	Country	Domain name	Since
Americas	Brazil	amazon.com.br	December 2012
	Canada	amazon.ca	June 2002
	Mexico	amazon.com.mx	August 2013
	United States	amazon.com	July 1995
Asia	China	amazon.cn	September 2004
	India	amazon.in	June 2013
	Japan	amazon.co.jp	November 2000
	Singapore	amazon.sg	July 2017
	Turkey	amazon.com.tr	September 2018
	United Arab Emirates	amazon.ae	May 2019
	Saudi Arabia	amazon.sa	June 2020
Europe	France	amazon.fr	August 2000
	Germany	amazon.de	October 1998
	Italy	amazon.it	November 2010
	Netherlands	amazon.nl	November 2014
	Spain	amazon.es	September 2011
	Sweden	amazon.se	October 2020
	United Kingdom	amazon.co.uk	October 1998
Oceania	Australia	amazon.com.au	November 2017

Source: https://en.wikipedia.org/wiki/Amazon_(company)

Amazon sells books in 19 marketplaces as of this writing. Suppose you plan to become an "international" bestseller—which is less competitive than becoming a US bestseller. In that case, you will want to identify and list categories targeted to those non-domestic markets specifically.

If you choose to distribute your book in predominantly English-speaking countries outside the US, then Canada, the UK, and Australia are the main markets. India and Germany are also solid markets for English titles.

Once you have uploaded the book, as an ebook or print book, Amazon takes up to three days to approve your book and have it become "live" on their site. Often this takes less than 24 hours—but during the early days of COVID, it took almost three weeks! So if you have a launch date in mind, don't assume that you can upload a day or two before your launch.

Some people teach the process of pre-sales or setting up your book for pre-order. I'm lazy (I'm not, but it sounds like something to say!) and don't like to go through any extra work if I can get the same or a better result without it! I also don't want to wait, and a pre-order strategy can take months! So I also don't teach or promote virtual or actual book signings, virtual or in-person book tours, book video trailers, scheduling TV or radio interviews, or reaching out in advance and bothering your friends and family. And I don't torture you with months and months of list-building.

The magic in co-authoring, using content from summits or podcasts, or joining our mastermind or membership program is that you reach an audience significantly more extensive than your own with zero extra effort, planning, organization, stress, and cost,

That's powerful! And a big relief!

Now it's time to market.

I've talked about "OP"ing things—not an original concept since using OPM, Other People's Money, has been bandied about forever. Now we talk about using OPAs (not IPAs)—Other People's Audiences.

The Dream 100 concept is simply a different way of suggesting you use OPA's. Using this strategy, your assignment is to identify people and companies who already have audiences full of your ideal customers. You then go through the arduous process of getting their attention (these idealized 100) and convincing them you have something of value they don't already have or can't easily find through one of their established connections.

IF they grant you access to their audiences, your task is to provide content that stands out amidst all the other people trying the same approach. Because these big influencers cycle through new content almost weekly, you become old news quickly.

Co-authoring a book, using content from your podcast or summit connections, or solo-authoring as part of our Million Dollar Method^{TM} Mastermind or Monthly Membership program, on the other hand, gets you in front of warm audiences with a strong introduction. It's like going to someone's home for a party, and the host validates your arrival by putting their arm around your shoulders, saying, "Hey, everyone, this is my dear and awesome friend. Come say hello!"

Not only are you seen as a highly trusted authority when you have that authentic connection with an influencer, but now you also get invited to join podcasts, FB live interviews, Clubhouse rooms, IG live chats, summits, and much more—not once, but over and over. Since you have more than one influencer in your close community, your reach and brand authority get engagement fast.

You won't simply appear in front of their audiences once and be replaced by someone next week. Instead, you have the opportunity to develop relationships with their audiences and return the favor; they get to add value for your audience as well.

Suppose you are a digital course creator, a consultant, a high-ticket coach, a podcast or summit host, an agency owner, an eCommerce owner, a network marketer, or a mission-and-success-driven entrepreneur. In that case, it is highly strategic to join a community to become a published best-selling author, replacing a piecemeal marketing strategy and saving you big on ad spend, time, and stress. Moreover, it's a lot of fun!

The Million Dollar Method^{TM} teaches you how to frame your business and content to serve your own and other people's audiences. This method helps you grow your influence, your audience, and your monthly revenue fast, with very little time, effort, or resources on your part.

Genuinely establishing relationships with your Million Dollar Mastermind, your Million Dollar Story community, or your co-authors leads to referral relationships and connections you wouldn't get on your own—or even be aware of. You avoid having to rely on increasingly expensive ad platforms and rapidly changing algorithms.

You also aren't forced into making your offer a commodity that competes on price. (Be sure to catch the Bonus module at the end of this book for actionable steps to take to increase both organic and paid traffic!)

What ROI can you expect as an author-entrepreneur?

Let's say your audience reach before becoming a published, best-selling author (combined between your email list and your presence on social media) is decent at 8000. You launch with nine other entrepreneurs who have similar audiences. On launch day, your combined audience reach is therefore 80,000 (ten author-entrepreneurs, each with an audience reach of 8000.)

Following Alex Charfen or Ryan Deiss's proven business strategy, you prospect, nurture, and convert your audience, and you deliver your product or service. Then you ascend them up your value ladder and retain them over their customer lifetime. This is the power of The Profit Pentagon^{TM}.

Before launch day, you only monetize 1% of your audience reach, so you have 80 paying customers. We will assume each customer has a current lifetime value to you of $10,000. Your projected business revenue is 80 X $10k = $80,000.

On launch day, your audience reach grows instantly from 8000 to 80,000, an increase of 1000% or an additional 72,000 sets of eyes paying attention to you.

Let's be ultra-conservative and forecast that you only convert a half-percent of those new prospects. (0.005 X 72,000) That's 360 new prospects who represent a lifetime value of $10,000 each. You now have projected new revenue of $360,000 with zero ad spend.

Imagine what happens when you are part of a community with influencers who each have an audience reach of 25,000 or higher!

WHO: James Golden! Case Study Success!

Million Dollar Story Author-Entrepreneur James Goldman

Let me highlight a member of our Million Dollar Story community. James Golden is the Founder and CEO of the Pavement Management Group and Chief Action Officer of JG3 Consulting. He got his start in pavement management working under a civil engineer and mentor at 19. What began as a part-time job performing roadway condition assessments turned into a 22-year career, plus a passion for helping municipalities across the US save taxpayer dollars, maximize their annual budget, and increase the conditions of their roadway networks. When he is not advocating for roadway preservation, James enjoys helping others in the constant pursuit of becoming the best version of themselves through personal and group coaching and his "Good to Goalden" podcast. The road to hitting your next level is just a click away. Get started today by joining James's free Facebook Group, *The Golden Collective*. James currently resides in Ohio with his wife Jamie and their five kids: Dillon, Jaden, Michaela, Caden, and Emersen.

MODULE 5: THE BEST SELLER LAUNCH FRAMEWORK

"Take your life and make it the best story in the world. This is not a dress rehearsal." Robin Arzón, Peloton

WHAT Result Will You Achieve?

"Jamie, look at me. Keep your eyes focused on mine, and let's just have a conversation, OK? And keep breathing!" Honestly, it was not a bad request from a good-looking, very fit man who was considerably younger than me, who also happened to be standing a mere two inches from me. If you zoomed in, you saw two adults standing quite closely, radiating a bit of intensity.

If you zoomed out, you also noted that we were very far off the ground, standing on a tiny platform attached to a tree that was moving quite a lot as the wind gusted strongly. We were both wearing harnesses and hard hats. His back was against the tree while mine was about an inch from … nothing! My next step was literally out into thin air—and I don't love heights.

It was my youngest son's birthday, and we were ziplining, so there I was with a bunch of fearless, laughing, screeching teenagers, girls and boys, having a blast up in the tree canopy on a clear, cold, gusty day. I usually adore watching trees dance in the wind. I simply wasn't in the habit of being in their top branches while they were doing so.

Clearly, I lived to tell the tale. I've never forgotten how grateful I was to that young man who didn't humiliate me, rush me, or bully me into taking that next step. And of course, once I did, it was absolutely exhilarating, and I remain proud of myself for literally stepping so far outside my comfort zone.

That's what a book launch feels like the first time, and in fact, I never lose those jitters. It's exciting in a way that can leave you a bit breathless. But, it's public, and once you jump, there's no going back.

But just like the ziplining adventure, there are procedures in place, along with experienced guides if you choose to use them, to ensure a successful outcome. Once you know the ropes (ha! I couldn't resist,) you will successfully move from stage to stage.

A book launch may have something else in common with ziplining. There is real work and preparation that goes into it, and yet the ride is fleeting and over very fast. The pride and the exhilaration last a long time after the event. You (and your business) will be forever changed from the experience, knowing what you have accomplished. But you'll want pictures to prove you were there!

WHY Does This Result Matter?

Let's have a frank conversation about Best Seller status for a minute.

There are different "Best Seller" lists: the New York Times, the Wall Street Journal, USA Today, Amazon, and a surprisingly large number of other lists where books rank. But these four are most familiar to people who aren't in the literary space; regular people appreciate the significance of ranking on these specific lists.

There are different rules and tracking methods, mostly around time periods, the number of books sold and by whom, their format, and a few other criteria, depending on which list you pursue.

While there is never a guarantee you will hit one, agencies that do this for a living get more experienced in gaming the system—or at least knowing how best to hedge your bets for desired results. The more assurance you want and the bigger the brand recognition you seek, the more it will cost you in marketing and project management.

While the Amazon Best Seller list is the "easiest" one to achieve because their algorithm counts how many books are sold every hour in multiple categories, there is still hefty competition on their platform, so becoming #1 remains a significant achievement.

Like it or not, it comes down to perception. If you have five knowledgeable, charismatic, sincere, strong, and lean fitness professionals to choose from to work with, but ONE states they are a published, Best Selling author (on any list,) that one now stands out as having increased authority and status. The others simply fade a bit into the background.

Staking the claim of Best Seller raises your visibility and trust factor for your prospective clients. It differentiates your brand, and people look at you differently.

There are three levels of "#1" on Amazon: #1 Hot New Release, #1 Best Seller, and the Best Seller banner. The banner is the hardest to obtain and therefore carries the most significance. Since the average reader is unaware of the nuances, achieving any one of these milestones helps your brand.

The lowest level is #1 Hot New Release, or sometimes simply #1 New Release

The subsequent sweet victory is #1 Best Seller, especially when you sit at #1 in the top 100 above some of the 'greats'! (Top 100 "Paid" means the book is not free to read.) This ranking is based on the volume sold.

The ultimate success is to receive the Best Seller Banner, which shows up in two ways—the first is illustrated here. As you scroll through a list of books, the banner appears next to those titles that have earned the ranking.

On the book's actual sales page, the Best Seller Banner will ONLY appear below the title section if, indeed, the book has ranked to the highest level. This level is based on distribution; how many unique purchases are made.

You can also achieve rankings in non-US markets, which are less competitive than the US market. Finally, you state you are an "international bestseller," which has quite the flare to it even though, in truth, it carries a bit less significance. In the grand scheme of things in most circles, those differences matter about as much as your high school grade in History matters to your current endeavors; even if you are an historian, the actual grade you earned years ago is irrelevant.

I don't dispute that people seem to know there is something 'more' to being a WSJ Bestseller than being an Amazon Best Seller. But suppose the results are roughly the same for your business strategy with a significantly smaller outlay of cash. In that case, it's unlikely to be pure ROI for your business that motivates you to pursue the loftier version of #1. Lucky for you, Million Dollar Story Agency also offers you the opportunity to become a USA Today or Wall Street Journal Best Seller in one of our anthologies, if that is the option you choose to pursue!

I also don't dispute that hitting #1 on Amazon is an algorithm game.

Becoming a published author—specifically a best-selling published author—is a strategic move. It is one tool of many for lead gen, brand awareness, and authority building.

In the Million Dollar Method^{TM}, it is also a relationship builder and audience multiplier.

It's the same as the 'pay to play' deal of getting on stages or in publications alongside big names. As long as you have clarity regarding your strategy and the outcomes you attach to that strategy, you won't be deterred by any naysayers, and you can be genuinely proud of your achievements.

HOW Do You Accomplish This Result?

Let's recap…

You have determined there is a strategic advantage to your

business, your brand, and your authority status to becoming a published author, and ideally, a #1 best-selling published author. Further, you have opted for the bundle approach in which you write your book and simultaneously create all the assets for your value ladder, including the funnel itself.

The first two steps involve writing and publishing.

You have investigated writing options—i.e., content production—available to you, which include the following:

1. Writing a traditional book—i.e., you are the sole author responsible for the content of roughly 200 pages or 50K-60K words by yourself. I use the term "writing" to mean you either write, hire a ghostwriter, or "talk/speak" the entire book, transcribe all that audio, and employ the editing team needed to transform the spoken word to an enjoyable-to-consume written word;

2. Writing a traditional book and either self-publishing or going through the time, effort, and opportunity-cost of working with a large, traditional publisher. (The same references to "writing" apply here as they did for 1.)

3. Producing a book from content you have obtained from your podcast.

4. Producing a book from content you have obtained from your summit.

5. Writing/speaking-recording one section up to a chapter in length to combine your content with other influential co-authors in a collaborative work; you either identify and recruit these influencers yourself or you participate with Million Dollar Story Agency to find them for you or with you. You also choose which list you'd like to target as a #1 Best-Seller: Amazon, WSJ, or USA Today.

6. Writing a traditional book—i.e., you are the sole author responsible for the content of roughly 200 pages or 50K-60K words by yourself—in which your book outline maps to your high-ticket course modules, and you use different formats of your book to produce the front-end of your funnel.

We discussed the logistics of the publishing step in Chapter 4. Your choices are to purchase any necessary software and learn to do this yourself or hire someone to do it all for you. Publishing ideally also involves a minimum of three formats: digital, print, and audio.

Lastly, there is marketing, the first step of which is to Launch your book.

The marketing of products, services, and books, by default, includes a conversation about your email list.

How extensive is your list?

If you have an engaged list and good copy for the subject line, an average email open-rate is roughly 18%. The email open-rate refers to the percentage of the total number of subscribers who open an email in a campaign. It varies by industry.

The next metric to note is the email click-to-open rate that looks at someone following a CTA (Call To Action) and clicking on a link within the body of the email. A general rule of thumb for a 'click to open' rate is about 14%.

So if you have an active email list of 1000 and 18% open your email, that means 180 people on your list read what you sent. Of those 180, 14%—or only 25 of them—will click on the link in the body that tells them to buy your book today.

If your goal is to sell 500 or 1000 books during your launch, and you're relying solely on your email list, your list size needs to range from 20,000 to 40,000!

While many people do have large lists, many course creators, consultants, speakers, coaches, digital agencies, other entre-preneurs, and small business owners do not. Nor do they necessarily have the time or other resources to build one—at least, not in time for their book launch!

While the standard advice is to drop a free lead magnet to build your list, even that does not produce guaranteed results—at least, not in the time frame or at a cost that meets your book launch needs.

If marketing is not your core strength, if it's new to you, if you haven't yet built a system for marketing whatever it is you do, this step can be almost more daunting than writing your book in the first place!

For book launches, I've seen instructions that feel equivalent to building a tiny house yourself when you aren't a builder. How hard can it be to do any or all of the following?

1. Plan a nationwide book tour at your own expense, complete with travel, food, venues, and local press.
2. Create a book movie trailer. The editing alone is a LOT, plus don't forget the importance of good copy.
3. Run Facebook ads and Amazon ads.
4. Stage pre-order campaigns that take months (and more months.)
5. Build interest by documenting every last step of your writing progress.
6. Drip out chapters.

7. Run contests and giveaways.

I'm overwhelmed—are you?

Importantly, none of that may include areas of core competency for you. It can be stressful, feel like rejection, and be a costly distraction from the work you do to serve your clients.

While Million Dollar Story Agency takes care of the book launch for you and with you, the Million Dollar Method™ lets you navigate this with minimal pain, cost, or distraction.

We can run a plan less than two weeks out that will consume less than five hours total of your time, and possibly less!

We're assuming that your endorsements and advance praise are in, your back cover copy is written, your title and subtitle are selected, your seven keyword strings and your ten categories for your ebook and your print book are selected in the US and any other markets you have chosen. We're also assuming your cover graphics are finalized, and you have a barcode for your ISBN.

Research and experience show that Tuesdays and Thursdays are the best days to launch your book.

Unless you work at a big publishing house, unfortunately, you won't be aware of what other books are launching on the same date as yours. Even they don't know their competitors' plans. Plus, you can't predict current events.

The truth is you may carefully choose your launch date only to discover you are competing for eyeballs with the launch of a book about a particular president, a specific global health event, or the latest celebrity or tragedy. It happens. For your launch purposes, those books are unlikely to be in similar categories to yours, so you should be OK!

We work across time zones, so we've found ourselves launching in a two-hour window covering twenty hours, 10 am in California to 6 am the following day in Australia. Time zones are so cool—actions are still limited to only two hours despite the twenty-hour range!

A word about categories—when a book is uploaded to Amazon, there are two spaces to list categories. Once the book is live on Amazon, you may contact Customer Service directly to add up to eight more categories. You can even delete the original two and replace them with up to a total of ten categories. These can be niched down, sometimes going four levels deep.

Categories   Choose up to two browse categories.

Set Categories

Choose up to two categories:

Choose categories (up to two):

⊞ Fiction
⊞ Nonfiction
⊞ Juvenile Fiction
⊞ Juvenile Nonfiction
⊞ Comics & Graphic Novels
⊞ Education & Reference
⊞ Literary Collections
☐ Non-Classifiable

Choose categories (up to two):

- ☐ Nonfiction
  - ⊞ Antiques & Collectibles
  - ⊞ Architecture
  - ⊞ Art
  - ⊞ Bibles
  - ⊞ Biography & Autobiography
  - ⊞ Body, Mind & Spirit
  - ☐ Business & Economics
    - ☐ General
    - ⊞ Accounting
    - ☐ Advertising & Promotion

Selected categories:

When you are in your KDP Account, you will click the button that says "Set Categories" and then see a condensed list of the primary categories. From there, click on a plus sign that opens a drop-down menu. Some sub-categories, but not all, will also have a plus sign that you can click to search the sub-sub-categories. Remember, you may only choose a total of two main categories during the process of uploading your book.

There is a strategy around choosing categories that may be less competitive. But while you may correctly claim that you hit #1 Best Seller, if someone asks, you do want to be able to stand by the categories in which you achieve #1. I could tell you horror stories…

Yes, it's Amazon's algorithm. Yes, it changes without warning. Yes, what you choose today may be different tomorrow.

Best Sellers Rank: #86,240 in Kindle Store (See Top 100 in Kindle Store)
  #8 in Financial Engineering (Kindle Store)
 #10 in Auctions & Small Business
 #20 in Home-Based Business Sales & Selling
Customer Reviews: ★★★★★ ⌄   50 ratings

Would you guess the subject of this book is fitness? No? It is…

Ideally, you want to rank in a category that at least closely reflects your area of expertise. You can—but it feels inauthentic to me—choose a category simply to rank. I don't recommend it, and the Million Dollar Story Agency does not practice it.

‹ Any Department

‹ Kindle Store

‹ Kindle eBooks

‹ Law

Intellectual Property

Communications

Entertainment

Patent, Trademark &
Copyright

For example, here's a screenshot of how categories appear to a Kindle buyer. You will find this drop-down menu on the left side of the page on Amazon. The categories here are as follows: Any Department > Kindle Store > Kindle eBooks > Law > Intellectual Property > and then within IP, you select one of those sub-niches.

IP is designed to protect the rights of innovators and inventions. IP around communications usually involves technology. So would you expect to see a book on marital relations taking #1 in Intellectual Property? No—but someone chose to take the word "communication" out of the context in which it was intended here.

One more example, and I'll leave it because you get the point: choose your categories with integrity, not just competition, in mind to aptly reflect the products and services you offer. I'm intentionally not naming books as my intent is not to embarrass anyone. I'm sure the content is valuable, but it feels like someone shelved loaves of bread in the diaper aisle; it just doesn't belong! In this case, I found a book about dealing with narcissist behavior earning #1 in email. Could I surmise that a narcissist might send a nasty email, and I'd need to know how to respond? Sure, and the book description says it's about taking back 'control of our boundaries' but... here's where the "email" sub-category appears:

‹ Any Department
  ‹ Kindle Store
    ‹ Kindle eBooks
      ‹ Computers & Technology
        Applications & Software
        Business
        Calculators
        E-mail
        Educational Software
        Mathematical & Statistical
        Natural Language Processing
        Office Software
        Personal Finance

Categories are worth spending a bit of time on because the purpose of your launch is for your book to hit Best Seller, and it will do so in up to three categories across both books and ebooks. It's part of the logistics of publishing while also being part of the strategy of marketing.

You've chosen your categories to reflect the business of the author (or businesses of the co-authors.)

You've selected your day, and then your date, as well as the window of time across time zones if you are launching simultaneously with Mastermind members, Community members, or co-authors.

When the book is published or uploaded, you also must select the price.

I have seen advice around having your book available for free—and advice to price it high and then drop it to free within 24 hours of the launch. I have seen more prominent names set their prices up to $14.99 for the kindle version. It's worth noting that trends change, so depending on when you read this book, do your due diligence (always, for everything) before deciding about pricing your book.

Million Dollar Story Agency has had consistent success setting the price for the kindle at 99 cents. Then once the launch is over, we raise that to market rates. Effectively this drives a potential book buyer to your funnel where they can pick the book up for free + shipping and enter your value-ladder.

Product details

ASIN : B0826C2294

Publisher : Wolf Tide Publishing (December 12, 2019)

Publication date : December 12, 2019

Language : English

File size : 3552 KB

Simultaneous device usage : Unlimited

Text-to-Speech : Enabled

Screen Reader : Supported

Enhanced typesetting : Enabled

X-Ray : Enabled

Word Wise : Enabled

Print length : 248 pages

Page numbers source ISBN : 1938953053

Lending : Enabled

Best Sellers Rank: #948,269 in Kindle Store (See Top 100 in Kindle Store)

#60 in User Generated Content (Kindle Store)

#72 in Home-Based Business Advertising

#75 in Podcasting & Webcasting

Customer Reviews: ★★★★★ ˅   56 ratings

The date of this screenshot is February 8, 2021—well over a year since the book was first published, and it is still in the Top 100 in 3 categories relevant to the authors' businesses.

Periodically we do additional marketing for all our authors' books and drop the book down to free for a finite promotional period. Because each author has links to opt-in pages within their chapters, our goal is eyeballs. Keeping our books in the Top 100 over time increases the help Amazon gives us.

The more readers who engage with your content, the more prospects will be introduced to your world for you to convert them into customers who enter your value ladder.

Finally, we put together a marketing funnel of freebies for launch day to make it an easy decision to spend one dollar. We ask each author to provide a link to an opt-in page, a title for their lead magnet, and a description of the result it gives. We create a funnel that lets people enter a members' area to access all the gifts, with each one leading to a page where an author collects an email address. The catch is that these freebies are ONLY available for 48 hours—on launch day and one additional day. And then we take it away. We offer urgency, and it's real!

If you have crafted a collaborative work of podcasters or sum-mit presenters, you can agree to follow the same strategy. Have each person whose content appears in the book also provide a free offer.

If you are writing a book entirely on your own and not using an agency like ours to help you launch and promote your book, consider reaching out to a group of other entrepreneurs you know who intend to write and see if you can coordinate your launches.

The power is in the numbers.

Remember our conversation around list building and our assessment that to sell 1000 books on launch day, you'd need a list of 40,000? If you and nine other networked influencers agree to a cooperative effort (or you've joined our community) and you each have a list of only 4,000, together you still reach 40,000 people simultaneously—with ZERO extra effort or expense on your part.

Think about that!

Of course, these days, your 4000 may come from TikTok, IG, FB groups, FB pages, Clubhouse, plus your email list, with no one platform having to be large. Years ago, I attended a Brendon Burchard conference when he was just getting started. He had us form groups of people whom each had a list of only 100 people. Five minutes later, when we parted ways, we'd come to an understanding that collectively, every one of us now had a list of 1000! The audience was targeted because we were all entrepreneurs, and it was warm because we could now vouch for each other!

Simple can be powerful, as long as it's executed!

One last word about nerves, launches, and speed.

Say you decide to launch between noon to 2 pm Central Time. Nothing will change on Amazon by 2 pm, regardless of how responsive your audience is. You—or your project manager or agency—will check again at 3... and 4... and maybe even 5 pm and still, NOTHING! Aaaagggghhhh!

And then—the wild ride begins, and it is SO exciting! Especially if there is a group of you with whom to celebrate. Suddenly you start to see #1 Hot New Releases showing up. And then maybe #1 Top 100's showing up.... And somewhere around midnight, if not a bit before, you may get to experience receiving the #1 Best Seller Banner in a hugely competitive category.

TAKE A SCREENSHOT!

Screenshot EACH success! It shows up a bit differently on mobile, so screenshot it there and on your desktop/laptop. And keep it for future reference.

The rankings will continue to come in and change over the next 24-48 hours. Depending on your marketing budget, any Facebook, Amazon, or other ads you've run, the press releases you've submitted, and the number of reviews you've received, you may stay at #1 for days or even a week or two. The more money you invest in promotion, the longer your ranking holds.

But even as you descend back to earth, know this.

Know that forever after this moment, YOU ARE a published best-selling author!

People will look at you differently.

Your brand will benefit.

Your authority will increase.

And if you've collaborated in any way with other influencers, their audiences will now know your name!

And you and they will forever have a powerful and incredible common bond, a foundation for future business!

If you want a copy of my free+shipping book funnel, click here.
https://www.milliondollarstory.co/funnel-template-free-plus-shipping-mdm-reader-bonus

WHO: Mark Stern! Case Study Success!

Million Dollar Story Author-Entrepreneur Mark Stern

Let me highlight a member of our Million Dollar Story community. Mark Stern is a serial entrepreneur and founder of Ultimate Authority, the Custom Box Agency, and Rough Streak Digital. Mark helps entrepreneurs build authority and scale their business with custom boxes and virtual events. Before becoming an entrepreneur, Mark was a top-ranked strategy consultant at Deloitte Consulting, the world's largest consulting firm. While at Deloitte, he was selected amongst the firm's 40,000+ US-based employees for a prestigious fellowship with the XPRIZE Foundation. He has spent the last decade working with Fortune 500 leaders across the retail, healthcare, fitness, beverage, and financial services industries. Mark holds an MBA from Duke University's Fuqua School of Business. He is a five-time Spartan Trifecta holder, SXSW Start-up Mentor, and lifetime lover of BBQ. Mark currently lives in Austin, Texas.

CLIENT DELIVERY & FULFILLMENT

MODULE 6: SYSTEMS & PROCESSES BLUEPRINT FOR SPEED

"Visualize something you want to accomplish today and get it done."
Robin Arzón, Peloton

WHAT Result Will You Achieve?

It was pitch black out, partly because it was still well before 5 am and partly because I felt like a mushroom existing in the dark for most of each day. That's Seattle in the winter. The headlights revealed something ahead on the road, right in the curve by the creek, but I couldn't make out what it was. Luckily the road by my house was a tiny one with virtually no traffic, especially at this hour, and the hard turn forced people to slow to a crawl.

I pulled over, got out, and was freshly awakened by the 35-degree drizzle. I got closer. It was a heron, or maybe a stork, or perhaps a crane. Birds, then and now, are not my area of expertise. It didn't move. Hmmm. That wasn't good, and I couldn't leave it there because someone else would drive this way eventually.

I took off my parka and laid it gently over the bird, being especially aware of covering the very long, hard beak. Gently I scooped it up, put it in the back seat, and turned around for home, aware that I was seriously messing with my schedule for the day—nothing like being stressed about time at o'dark thirty.

Once home, I planned to wait until business hours and call the wildlife rescue folks. Because I had dogs, cats, and kids, I figured the safest place for it would be the least-used bathroom. Carefully and slowly, I carried it into the sleeping house, up the stairs, down the hall, and into the small bathroom. I decided to put it in the tub in case it made a mess.

Holy sh*#! Imagine my shock when—as I bent over, placed it down, and slowly pulled my parka from its body—it gracefully and slowly stood up as I did. Between its legs and its neck, we found ourselves staring at each other inches apart. That was one tall bird!

I recovered from my surprise, backed out, closed the door, and quickly put a BIG sign on the door saying DANGER, KEEP OUT! I didn't need curious kids or pets making the injured animal feel as if it needed to defend itself when it was bigger than they were!

The bird had a happy ending; it was successfully rehabbed and released.

That one day, my schedule didn't fare as well.

My routine was to hit the grocery store once a week on a weekday before five AM to have the store to myself—plus all the industrious re-stockers. I'd be home and have everything unloaded and put away by 6ish in time to walk the dog.

In winter, in Seattle, walking the dog required the time to put on full foul-weather gear. I learned the hard way that if I only wore a raincoat, the water would run off it and soak my legs. (I also realized if I tucked my pants into my boots, my socks got wet as the water drained from my pants, but I digress.) The point being, it took extra time and attention just to walk the dog!

As many parents can attest to, managing a household is a lot of work. Add in pets to care for and a killer commute in a big urban area, getting kids to school and afterschool events, and myself to and from work didn't just happen. It took systems, processes, and planning for desired outcomes. Sometimes things happened to disrupt it—like a 5'8" bird hurt in the middle of the road—but overall, all the planning made things easier and more conducive to my sanity most of the time.

Anyone who's managed processes or people—maybe especially people—knows you want a plan in place to reach desired results with the least amount of time, pain, effort, and cost.

Working with busy entrepreneurs with demands on their time and focus requires an easy-to-follow-and-navigate process.

There is no shortage of tools, apps, trackers, and project management software. Choose what works for you and decide how you will deploy it. Do you have to learn how to use it? Teach others how to use it? Is it updated often? Is it cost-efficient for what you get from it and for your organizational size?

Do be sure to not only narrow your selections down, so you're not overloaded through attempting to be more efficient, but for software solutions of any kind, pay attention to the monthly subscription fees plus automatic renewals. They can add up in a hurry, and if you aren't even using them, there is certainly no point in paying for them.

A thought on time management... we are not actually managing time.

Time doesn't alter course. We are managing ourselves moving through time. All the tools are there for us to manage ourselves and our to-do lists, to prioritize, to track, to measure, to adjust. We get more efficient at managing ourselves to increase our productivity and improve outcomes—including feeling less stressed and more in alignment. But we never manage time.

WHY Does This Result Matter?

The Million Dollar Method^TM isn't merely a method to write a book. Many excellent programs help you learn to write, start to write, finish writing, and organize your writing.

Suppose you want to write in a specific genre, such as fiction, screenplays, or children's books. In that case, there are yet more courses to teach you sentence structure, character development, and even illustration to accompany the text.

Think of the Million Dollar Method^TM more like Harvard Business School.

Your colleagues (in your membership community, your mastermind community, or your co-authors) will have been carefully screened and selected for their shared passion for excellence plus diverse talent and backgrounds.

You will learn skills.

You will work to achieve a result (degree/book.)

More importantly, you will build relationships and establish a network that will open doors for a lifetime. You will be elevated simply by the company you keep.

The process establishes a foundation for exceptional, flourishing business growth.

Graduating from HBS isn't the endpoint; it's just the beginning.

Becoming a published Best Selling author with MDM isn't just about the book.

You can get a grad degree in business from lots of different universities. I'm proud of my MBA from Arizona State University. Still, my brother, an HBS alumnus, will remind me, "It's not the same." You can learn to write and self-publish, or you can pay to get your book written and published from many programs.

Becoming a published Best Selling author with the Million Dollar Method^{TM} goes well beyond the book. Our program exists to build your brand and build your business efficiently, so that with one effort you strengthen every piece of The Profit Pentagon^{TM}.

Joining influential author-entrepreneurs elevates your status while significantly increasing your distribution—your audience reach—with no extra advertising dollars required.

Joining successful, experienced entrepreneurs as part of our community or as co-authors opens doors to future JV relationships (Joint Ventures) and Affiliate offers, perhaps even partnerships. At the very least, next time you need to ask, "Whom do you know...?" you will have multiple well-connected leaders who will respond to your request as a priority.

(Think of this another way. If 'Cash is King' in the business world, Connection is the King's currency, and Content makes up the King's army!)

Once the book itself is written—without your having to write if writing isn't your strength—we move to marketing.

Most first-time authors have zero awareness that marketing is a much bigger mountain to climb than producing a book. And most programs catering to would-be authors leave you without any marketing support at all. Even the big publishing houses provide very little marketing. And while Amazon effectively has "limitless" shelf-space globally, once there, you compete against the two-million plus titles published annually.

You want help with the marketing side of your book for you to get reviews and to rank. Remember, having 'Best Seller' attached to your name as a published author not only transitions your status from expert to authority, it is one of the qualifiers—along with good press—for obtaining a Verified Blue Checkmark from Instagram and Facebook.

Being a best seller invites PR, while the blue checkmark has you viewed as a celebrity with tens of thousands of followers. Now you have diversified for another monetization stream.

Do you see now that marketing your book is essential?

HOW Do You Accomplish This Result?

So what systems and processes does the Million Dollar Method^{TM} follow?

I wish I had a picture from when I wrote my first book because I remember it vividly.

I wrote ten "hooks" that became my chapter titles. I had ten stacks of books piled like kids' blocks for research for each of the ten topics. I lay on the floor on my belly perusing books, noting references, and writing. For months I wouldn't let anyone in the room, so they didn't disturb my 'system!' I wrote it all by hand. My gosh, the whole process was arduous and slow!

Now, in-house, we use spreadsheets with multiple tabs for every phase of the process, from prospecting to writing, publishing, launching, and ongoing marketing.

Author-entrepreneur facing we use a combination of some cool software that makes things stupid-simple, Trello boards, automated emails, a private FB group, a FB Messenger thread, and Voxer.

And we move FAST! There is no reason for it to take longer than 90 days at most from first committing to the process to being a published best-selling author to having a finished book and your next offer or re-branding offer complete!

There are programs out there to "write your book in a weekend" or become a "four-hour author" and other ultra-expedited promises. It's important to consider WHY you are writing a book and what RESULT you want the process to achieve. Also dive into what exactly is being promised. It's not always quite what it seems on the surface.

I have found that some of these programs deliver only an outline (remember my book piles?) and once you leave your weekend event, you still have to write the whole book.

Sometimes, the "book" you produce is less than 50 pages long—which I suppose technically could be thought of as a book, so they aren't lying exactly.

Other programs deliver an ebook in those short time frames. Still, it may be another year before the print version shows up, which is fine as long as you get something that strategically works for you and delivers business results that matter.

Perhaps you shell out $1.5 million to a major publishing house (for real) to become a New York Times Best Seller... or close to $100K to become a Wall Street Journal and USA Today Best Seller, but then learn that the use of a ghostwriter or the assistance of a publicist is billed separately in addition to what you've already paid—and even on *those* lists it's the ebook only that trips the algorithm, at those prices! (Million Dollar Story Agency offers you a much better deal, btw, if you choose to participate in one of our USA Today or WSJ anthologies.)

Just understand the details behind the hooks—the bodacious promises and program titles designed to lure you in—and cross-reference them against why you want to write a book in the first place.

Suppose your salary plus stock options, endorsements, or speaking engagements is more than $25M per year. In that case, it's almost an afterthought to spend a few million to drip the tidbit at your next cocktail party that you are now an NYT Best Seller. It's all relative. As long as you have clarity around the results you want and do your due diligence, you'll be fine.

The Million Dollar Story Agency offers a Done-For-You service that delivers the three basic formats for the broadest audience distribution: an ebook and a print book within 90 days and an audiobook within another 60-90 days. The audiobook lags because it typically takes 30-45 days for editing, followed by 30-45 days for Amazon's ACX review process.

We provide all the necessary writing and publishing services, beginning with a hybrid ghostwriting service, so you don't even have to write if, as Bartleby says, you prefer not to.

We include content editing, copy editing, and proofreading.

We provide interior formatting, front and back cover graphics, an ISBN, and a boutique publishing imprint.

And, of course, project management to keep everything on a short, fast timeline.

Next, we orchestrate the marketing so that you, or you and

your co-authors, achieve Best New Release and #1 Best Seller.

Then we go beyond that to ensure you receive the differentiated Amazon Best Seller Banner.

All three happen in categories relevant to you.

Finally, while being an International Best Seller deserves respect, being a Best Seller in the most competitive market globally, the US, says more. We make sure you are #1 in the world!

To accomplish this, we build the marketing funnel, manage the free offers, handle the SEO for the subtitle, the back cover copy, and the keyword strings. We carefully select ten categories (not just two) in the US, plus different ones abroad, to improve your chances with Amazon's ever-changing and always carefully guarded secret algorithms.

We handle Amazon reviews, Amazon ads, and press releases. We assist you in creating or updating your author page. The greats don't stop with one book—they proudly claim to be the author of multiple bestsellers. It doesn't serve anyone for you to have the mindset that if you've already written one book, you don't "need" to write another one or participate in another collaborative effort.

We provide the email copy and social media templates to share across multiple platforms simultaneously—talk about exponential reach with minimal effort! Especially if you have delegated these tasks to your assistant.

Besides providing your initial content based on the framework we provide, you barely have to interact with the project at all! For far less than a monthly outlay for Facebook management and ads, you will reach a vast audience of targeted warm prospects—warm because you are now cohorts of people they already trust for solutions.

However, if you want to be more hands-on, or aren't ready for the price point of Million Dollar Story Agency's Done-For-You services, instead, avail yourself of the 'done with you' Million Dollar Method^{TM}. You can access all our Systems & Processes Blueprint for Speed in our MDM Mastermind, complete with weekly group sessions plus weekly Q&A sessions.

In our Done-With-You Mastermind and our DIY Monthly Membership options, we also help you with both your marketing launch funnel and your value ladder offers and funnel. If you choose to, you create your course or mastermind while crafting your book, bundling your results; all your business assets are complete with one effort in one limited timeframe!

Additionally, our services can include identifying and securing influential co-authors for you if you choose this option, targeting either Amazon or the bigger lists.

The program that is right for you all depends where you fall on the scale of more money than time/time than money and how developed your business infrastructure is or is not.

First, know WHY you want to be a #1 best selling author and WHAT result will define your success. Next, be clear on what you gain when you develop your book content and business assets simultaneously. Then choose HOW to best accomplish your goals.

What will being a published best selling author do for your brand and authority?

What will author-entrepreneur relationships with Influencers do for your business?

What will expanding your audience reach tenfold in just two hours do for your lead generation?

What will delivering value across all consumable formats of digital, print, and audio mean for accessibility by those in pain, with problems you can solve now?

How will you make a difference and contribute a more significant impact to your colleagues and co-authors, your readers and audience, your prospects, and theirs?

Below is an example of a Trello board for a collaborative anthology project with co-authors.

WHO: Dr. Grace Lee! Case Study Success!

Million Dollar Story Author-Entrepreneur Dr. Grace Lee

Let me highlight a member of our Million Dollar Story community. She helps entrepreneurs create, convey, and convert their offers so that they can monetize their knowledge or expertise online. Her YouTube channel has 2.4+ Million views and she adds 10,000 new subscribers monthly. That generates $80k+ new monthly business revenue. Dr. Grace Lee is the founder of Mastery Insights, host of *Inciting Influence* and *Career Revisionist* podcasts, and creator of a practical, business & career channel on YouTube. Dr. Grace is sought after as a speaker and trainer in the areas of sales, business development, career development, public speaking, mindset, and neuroscience. Through her coaching firm, Mastery Insights, she is dedicated to enabling professionals to take their education, expertise, and experiences, and (1) turn it into a passion for profit online, or (2) leverage it to create greater income and impact in a meaningful career path. She has trained hundreds of people from 10+ countries all over the world. Using her expertise from her PhD in neuroscience, Dr. Grace's methods empower you to discover a different way of thinking to take the guesswork out of what to do next so you can grow fast. **tubecelebritycodex.com**

MODULE 7: DELEGATING THE DETAILS

"Strong enough to be self-reliant and brave enough to ask for help."
Robin Arzón, Peloton

WHAT Result Will You Achieve?

Several years ago, I found myself in a position where I had to help someone sell a house in another state. They were experiencing health complications which added urgency to the situation. I already had my hands full, so I did the only other thing I could; I asked for help.

I did some research, narrowed a selection down, and interviewed three realtors. I chose one. I explained my time frame and logistics issues. She was not only a great project manager, but she also had a strong network. We essentially formed a partnership with a mission to sell a house fast with minimal effort in a defined price range.

First, she brought someone in to assess the contents of the house. Some went to auction, and she sent a check minus a percentage. Some went to Goodwill. What wasn't salvageable went to the landfill. Within a week, the house was empty.

Next, she identified carpet cleaners, window cleaners, and general house cleaners for my review. Based on her recommendations and their availability, I made selections. They got to work and did an excellent job making the old look new and fresh.

Meanwhile, a handyman came in to address normal wear and

tear—a faucet that dripped, a light switch that didn't work, a kitchen drawer that stuck, a bulb in the fridge that needed replacing. And while details inside were attended to, the outside landscaping received overdue attention for improved curbside appeal. The entire exterior was pressure-washed.

The realtor checked with me every step of the way, asked for and received approval, sent receipts, and kept communication clear and prompt. Within a few short weeks of the initial agreement, the house was ready to be listed. She started scheduling open houses. She worked the offers, handled the inspection, and kept the activity level high.

The house sold with an all-cash offer above the minimum that had been set in less than 90 days from my first conversation with her. I responded to phone calls, texts, and emails and provided the funding. That was it. Even the closing did not happen in person in deference to the unwell homeowner headed for a nursing home.

I felt like I'd moved a mountain, yet the whole experience was exceptional because of the realtor, her network, her project management, and her team.

It's been a benchmark for me since. "If I can do all that in 84 days, what else can I do?" But in reality, the only thing I did was choose the right person for the job; her network and teams did the rest.

WHY Does This Result Matter?

Million Dollar Story Agency has produced multiple books for multiple entrepreneur experts, 100% of whom are now published Best Selling authors.

Do you recall The Profit Pentagon^{TM} for your business?

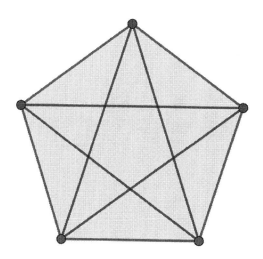

- Lead Generation & Prospecting.

- Lead Nurture & Relationship building.
- Lead Conversion & Sales.
- Client Delivery & Fulfillment.
- Client Client Retention & Ascension.

Let's also refresh your memory about the Million Dollar Method™ incorporating SEAS—Speed, Ease, Assets, and Status.

Delegate in the focus areas to yield calm SEAS.

For example, Chris Baden and Sean Malone run Sales Ascenders and are co-Founders of FlowChat™. Their system allows you to delegate your prospecting to one or more Virtual Assistants. The goal is to fill your calendar with sales calls.

When your calendar is full, you can then hire salespeople to speak with your prospects, understand their pain points, learn where their roadblocks are and what they've tried previously. These calls uncover whether or not this is a client with whom you want to work. Are they excuse-or-solution-oriented? Are they in the habit of investing in themselves? Are they focused on where they are going with a plan in place to get there? Do they need some help along the way?

Now it comes to delivery, and we've broken that down into four phases:

- Producing (writing)
- Publishing
- Marketing
- Monetizing

You can produce all of the content for one book yourself; as long as it is a non-fiction business-centric book, you can use the Million Dollar Method^{TM} to get it done. The best part of choosing this option is that you can use it to rebrand your offer or create an additional offer, pairing your book with your new course or mastermind and creating both with just one effort!

This is a traditional book with a twist of powerful strategy. While it meets the older, more conventional expectation when people talk about "having a book inside them" or saying they've "always wanted to write a book" it goes beyond that in clarity and focus, producing ROI for your business. The great news is there is absolutely no rule anywhere that says you can only write one book or only write one type of book.

You can repurpose content from podcasts or summits.

This gives you a few advantages. You don't have to write 50K to 60K words yourself. And you have a ready-made group of influencers with high-value content. The challenge here is surmountable but should not be ignored. Find editors skilled in content/developmental editing, copy editing, and proofreading. The key here is to create a good flow within each section and across all sections to produce a coherent, consumable, high-quality end product.

Your other option is to gather a group of influencers with the express purpose of creating content for your book. These influencers can center around a theme, an area of expertise, a common interest, or they may have complementary roles around a supply chain or ecosystem.

For example, perhaps you are writing a book focused on early childhood development because your area of expertise is homeschooling. Your authors may be experts in Montessori education, childhood nutrition, meditation for children, foreign language instruction for children, exercise and sports for preschoolers, music and the arts, behavior and social skills, or help for parents. In other words, your book can be a one-stop-shop for your reader and prospect, filled with helpful information and resources.

You may fall into the camp of having already written and published a book some time ago, and now that you know more, you realize that book could have done more. Or perhaps you've written most of your manuscript already and now feel it would be great to have support for the publishing, marketing, and monetizing portions. If either of these describes you, opt for our monthly membership or our 12-week master-mind.

HOW Do You Accomplish This Result?

Delegate the project management.

When you ask the right question, you ask "Who?" not "How?"

Who can run a project for you?

Call them your Executive Assistant, your Project Manager, your Author Project Manager, or your OBM—online business manager.

Regardless of title, this is the person whose duties include first helping to create the deadlines and then following up to make sure they are met. They must be excellent communicators! They must be "chaos coordinators" with an eye towards minimizing chaos. They must be reasonably unflappable, and you must trust them because they will be dealing with various personalities. They must be aligned with your mission, and you must like each other and respect each other. Yes, they work for you. But you will talk to them daily and they will be on the front lines, speaking with your voice.

The challenge with running a project with multiple contributors or multiple vendors is that there are numerous failure points. You know the saying about a chain only being as strong as its weakest link. If you don't set the project up correctly, one person can hold the entire schedule hostage if they don't respect delivery dates.

Of course, always build fudge factors into your timeline because it is 100% guaranteed life will happen to someone at different points along the timeline. That's a given.

Make sure you have contingencies built in, which may include replacing an author with someone on your waiting list or a vendor with someone in your Rolodex—with no refund to the person or entity who put the project in jeopardy.

That's at your discretion, of course. Sometimes people do have unforeseen things happen and deserve accommodation. But sometimes, their commitment to the project is superficial, and that's not fair to your reputation. Just be sure to have language, in any agreements, that describes the instances in which they won't be reimbursed—or published, if this applies. And then make sure they've signed the contract.

Actually, making sure the contracts are signed is a job for your project manager!

It is essential, in my view, to keep your in-house team tight. There is no point in generating $83K per month—the run rate needed for $1M per year—if your expenses equal or exceed that amount. Your goal should be to have a genuinely healthy profit margin. If you follow Mike Michalowicz and his *Profit First* methodology, you might aim for a 40-50% margin. If you follow other examples, you may get close to an 80% profit margin—the more significant your payroll and over-head, the lower your margins. And don't forget about taxes!

We use Trello boards, Google docs, Google calendars, Zoom, Calendly, Canva, and some excellent CRM software. Of course, there is a lot of project and team management soft-ware to choose from: AirTable, ClickUp, Basecamp, Process Street, Jira—and many more. It truly depends on the size of your team, the size of your budget, and what best meets your company's needs. You want to be agile without overcompli-cating anything.

We have daily and weekly check-ins.

Know that there are different segments of the project along with various components of the team. Your project manager should have a calendar to communicate all deadlines to team members, vendors (and any additional authors,) and their assistants. The PM has the big picture and the responsibility to make each person deliver at the right time.

Think of it as orchestrating a typical family evening. If you are all to have a great meal together, someone has to first decide the menu, being sensitive to anyone's special dietary requirements. Then the ingredients must be purchased, maybe as part of your routine weekly shopping or specifically just for that day or meal. Everyone needs to know when to be home for dinner, so they show up on time. Pretend it's pre-Covid, and you have to coordinate rides home from work, practice, or daycare for multiple people. You have to allow for showers, homework, walking the dog, cleaning up after the meal, and maybe even a late game. There are a lot of moving parts, right?

In our case, we might begin as early as the lead gen and prospecting phase. If you have a sales funnel, you may have the following pages: optin page, VSL page (video sales letter), application page, calendar page, order page, confirmation page, or some combination of these. The links need to work, email integration has to work, email sequences have to be written, pixels need to be on the right pages, and follow-up needs to be automated for those who register for a call. If the calls go to a sales team, that coordination has to be managed as well.

If you are running ads or driving paid traffic to your funnel, all those steps need to be set up and working. Presumably, you have hired an agency or media buyer for this part, so your

PM needs only to coordinate with them, making sure they've received all the assets they need to do their work.

Perhaps you are using an organic traffic method with VA's (virtual assistants) or appointment setters reaching out for you on IG, LI, or other social media platforms. Or you have a chatbot set up, and someone manages that for you. In the case of the VAs, you have metrics that they and you track daily, weekly, and monthly to meet sales goals. Someone needs to coordinate with those VAs daily to make sure they are clear on their tasks, and they are following through adequately.

Next, if co-authors/podcast/summit participants are onboarded, there is a process to follow—adding them to an email sequence or a specific group messenger thread, having them review and sign a contract, verbally committing and signing that they understand the deliverables and scope of the project. We have deliverables, and so do they, and we rely on each other for successful project completion.

Your project manager routinely checks that all project management assets are in place, that all vendors (and/or author-entrepreneurs) know what is expected of them next, and reaches out to anyone who seems to need support.

The project manager also interfaces with the various team members who make magic behind the scenes, including different editing teams, graphic designers, SEO experts, Amazon ad folks, PR folks, and layout and design experts. Each layer has contingencies, so it's crucial someone has their finger on the pulse of the total project. The graphic designer can't design a spine until the final page count is in. The final page count can't happen until all endorsements are received, and all final edits are complete. Edits can't even begin until content is received.

1	new title and subtitle selected based on SEO
2	solicit 2-3 endorsements/advance praise for current volume
3	need overall timeline from day 1 through completion
4	need checklist for authors
5	need checklist for EA/support
6	need project plan with all deliverables assigned to people with dates due
7	need their chapter recordings transcribed
8	need their transcripts converted to google docs
9	chapter template with word count
10	get graphic designer to create covers: ebook with and without BS, print book with and without BS, audiobook with and without BS
12	folders created, files uploaded to correct folders, folders shared appropriately
13	authors write from their own transcript - or editors "ghostwrite" from transcript
14	first drafts reviewed and edited for FLOW, redundancy, readability
15	individual chapter drafts shared with authors
16	full doc assembled - add quotes to chapters, add bios to end of doc, add headshots to end of doc, update TOC
17	full doc assembled - leave space for endorsements, add prologue, add epilogue
18	check that all links in doc work
19	add endorsement to doc as received
20	all final edits approved by authors

21 doc to interior formatting

22 back cover copy written, to layout & design (for book description) and to graphics person

23 key word phrases selected/SEO

24 categories selected (10 for ebook, 10 for print book, US markets, international mkts)

25 get graphics to interior layout and design

26 get ISBN to graphics person and interiror formatting, get barcode

27 ebook uploaded to Amazon (watch review time!)

28 once fully formatted ebook is published to Amazon, distribute digital copy (PDF) to authors as fully formatted ebook is one of their deliverables

29 once book is officially listed on Amazon, contact KDP support to add all 10 updated categories for ebook

30 once book is officially listed, send instructions to authors to create their author pages (or link new book to their existing page)

31 print book uploaded to Amazon - once it is there, authors have access to purchase wholesale books at cost (print + shipping + tax)

32 follow up with authors on narration of chapter

33 get raw audio to audiobook editor

34 once audio files are edited, they go to PM for uploading on ACX - review period is 30 days

35 get all edited files to authors - they have an fully edited/formatted audiobook as a deliverable

36 Press releases written, submitted to PR service for launch of ebook

37 ebook listed for Verified reviews

38 ebook lised for Amazon ads running to it

39 collect all components for freebie offer stack, update funnel, check pixels: (author graphic and title on page 1, updated book link on page 2, updated everything X 10 in members area

Imagine having ALL of this on your shoulders alone. Oh, heck no!

Know that you will delegate to your PM. They, in turn, will oversee some or all of the following:

- Exceptional customer service—communication with and support for your clients, the author-entrepreneurs, and/or their point person
- Funnel builder/tech support—for prospecting, for launch day and/or your value ladder offer
- Copywriter/email support—for prospecting, for launch day

- Facebook ads/Amazon ads agency—for prospecting, for launch day
- Editing team—developmental, content, copy, final proofs
- Graphic Designers—front and back covers, coordinate with copywriter, SEO
- Interior formatting, layout & design
- Publisher—ISBN, barcode (coordinate with graphic designer, interior designer,) price setting, country settings, author pages, book description, book reviews
- SEO/SEM—Category selection, keyword string selection, back cover copy
- PR—write & distribute press releases, update best-seller successes
- Ongoing publicity and ads for books, for authors
- Course or Mastermind delivery if you choose to bundle your book efforts with business-building

The last part is monetizing.

Be sure all the links in the text work. They will be live in the digital version but will need to be easy to follow for the print version and easy to say in the audio version. This will be a source of evergreen lead gen. Each time the book is promoted, someone new will learn about you and enter your world.

Be certain to coordinate with any Mastermind members, your Million Dollar Story community, and any co-authors to host each other on podcasts and in summits. See what affiliate offers you might share with each other's audiences. Know what skill sets they have as you might find a great way to do a joint venture in the future. When you need a referral, ask our network first!

Finally, recognize that the phenomenal power in becoming a Best Selling published author is in the increased influence, brand awareness, list size, visibility, audience reach, authority, and status you receive because of how people now see you.

These, in turn, lead to more invitations to speak, appear on podcasts, participate in summits, co-author books, and write guest articles.

These, in turn, grow your authority even more.

You have entered into an upward growth spiral. As your influence grows, your audience grows. Now you have more opportunities than ever before to monetize, not through book sales, but through having people enter your value ladder beginning with your book.

As your authority grows, you naturally affiliate with other influencers, so your reputation as a VIP grows, making you increasingly in demand. Make sure you have a great OBM or COO on board to help coordinate everything in your business house!

WHO: Chris Baden! Case Study Success!

Million Dollar Story Author-Entrepreneur Chris Baden

Let me highlight a member of our Million Dollar Story community. Chris is typically thinking about building three things at any given moment: a life-long marriage, a world-impacting family, and multi-million dollar businesses. In the last five years, Chris has been an equity partner in three different businesses in three different industries (Insurance, e-Comm, and Software) that grossed at least $1 Million per year in revenue. None of this would have been possible if it wasn't for one essential skill he developed... Prospecting! Chris often refers to it as Purpose Driven Prospecting, which emphasizes building new quality connections for maximum lifetime value. For example, Chris Baden and Sean Malone run Sales Ascenders.

Their system allows you to delegate your prospecting to one or more Virtual Assistants. The goal is to fill your calendar with 10+ sales calls per week organically. When your calendar is full, you can then hire salespeople to speak with your prospects, understand their pain points, learn where their roadblocks are and what they've tried previously. These calls uncover whether or not this is a client with whom you want to work. Are they excuse-or-solution- oriented? Are they in the habit of investing in themselves? Are they focused on where they are going with a plan in place to get there? Do they need some help along the way? And now FlowChat software is the exact foundation you need to grow your prospecting exponentially! Chris is a father of three and outside of business, Chris is an avid golfer—and fun fact… he and his wife, Beth, competed on the hit TV Show "American Ninja Warrior" multiple years in a row! If you are interested in working with Chris, connect with him here—*SalesAscenders.com* or FlowChat.com.

CLIENT RETENTION & ASCENSION

MODULE 8: CELEBRATE BRAND STATUS, AUTHORITY, & SALES

"Chin up. Crown on. If you give up now, what was it all for?" Robin Arzón, Peloton

WHAT Result Will You Achieve?

It's time for some future-casting. If you read this book, or better yet, if you enroll in our USA Today anthology program, our 12-week Mastermind, or our month-to-month continuity program, you want to be clear on WHY you will write a Best Selling book to build your brand.

How is becoming a best-selling published author going to help you grow your influence, audience reach, and revenue fast?

Great question! Let's dive in!

"I'm waking up today just laughing, thinking of all the people in

my life that knew me, to hear I'm now a published best-selling author. My mom, passed away at 54 from melanoma c in 2004, is looking down at me from heaven hysterical laughing. Student I was not. @Jamie Wolf you are making dreams come true, making an impact on our lives, helping us make an impact on other lives. This is just wonderful. I'm so happy I said yes to you." EB

"Just pointing this out then I'm going to bed…. All of our names rank higher than Jeff Bezos at the moment in the Entrepreneurship category… On his own platform. Let that sink in, soak it up and let's all get back to work and close out the week strong." JG

"That is hysterical!! We beat Russell!!" LW

"My kids just got home and told me they're proud of me" CL

"This is all so exciting!!! Honored to be part of this group." LW

"OMG this is AMAZING!" IM

"I just can't get enough! This is so cool" OU

"Awesome everyone. This is exciting. The best part of this is I've had people reach out to me with excitement saying they get it. We are making an impact, that's powerful stuff. Get used to the words: Best Selling Author next to your name! EB

WHY Does This Result Matter?

Let's reflect on what you will accomplish using the Million Dollar Method^{TM}.

When you write the right book strategically for your business, you plan to achieve the following results:

An evergreen *Lead Gen/Prospecting* tool

A *Lead Nurture* system, so prospects get to Know, Like & Trust you

A *Lead Conversion* system so cold leads are warmed up as they read your book, so conversion rates go up, and conversion costs go down

A Done For You Business *Client Delivery/Fulfillment* system: Sales Funnel + Assets of free lead magnet, F+S book, Bump Offer, and First OTO (your course or mastermind)

*Client Retention and Ascension/*Upsell system with a strategically written book bringing clients into your value ladder who become raving lifelong fans

A completed *ebook*

A completed *print book*

A completed *audiobook*

A *Published* book

A *Launched* book

Best Seller status as a published author

A Process to *Monetize* based on your book

BRAND awareness

Elevated *AUTHORITY*

Personal Fulfillment because you DID IT!

You have become a published, best-selling author & you have grown your influence, audience, and revenue fast—now you are positioned to start or grow your movement, make a difference, impact lives, and leave your legacy.

You choose to produce a best-selling book as a focused and strategic business decision to re-brand or brand to give you one more highly recognized and effective tool to expand on your existing business from the outset. Becoming a published best-selling author enhances your ability exponentially to do more of whatever you want to do most to positively affect the largest audience possible. Because you have strategically chosen to join our community, repurpose your podcast or summit content, or co-author, you immediately multiply your audience ... which means the people who need your help now don't have to wait to find you!

There are so many reasons to celebrate your accomplishment; the excitement and pride you feel celebrating WITH others—your community, your team, your co-authors if applicable, your family, your clients, and your audience—is an AH-MAZING FEELING!

One reason you are determined to become a best-selling entrepreneur-author is to transition from expert to authority. Once you've produced and published content, you market and then monetize. You get invited to podcasts, summits, speaking engagements, to do joint ventures, to do affiliate offers, and more. You are firmly establishing your brand status. As a best-selling author, you now are on your way to obtaining that blue checkmark on Instagram (and Facebook.)

Becoming a best-selling published author and becoming verified on Instagram are both strategies that differentiate you from your competitors. Both give you and your brand better credibility, strengthen the perception on social media that you are trustworthy (which you back up by delivering high integrity and authenticity,) and provide a more robust search presence. IG reserves its blue checkmarks for the "authentic presence of a notable public figure, celebrity, or global brand." **That's you!**

When prospects see you as a best-selling published author and see you are verified, they know they can trust you and that you've done something red-carpet worthy. Both should be part of your overall marketing strategy because both improve your conversion rates for monetization.

Becoming a best-selling published author is note-worthy in the press. You can and should have press releases for your book. As you get invited to podcast shows, summits, and speaking engagements, make sure there is press around these events: the higher your authority and visibility, the greater your opportunities to contribute valuable content across platforms. Whether YouTube, Clubhouse, or TikTok is your thing, you'll get more views. Share your articles on Twitter. When IG sees you are a Best Selling author and you have a strong presence on other platforms, it expedites your verification process.

The beauty of co-authoring or repurposing summit or podcast content into a collaborative anthology is the activity elevates your status and exponentially increases your distribution with zero extra effort on your part. It also creates results that come full circle: best seller yields more press which yields more status which yields more marketing opportunities which yields more authority which yields more marketing opportunities which yields more monetization which yields more noteworthy news—and the snowball builds and accelerates!

HOW Do You Accomplish This Result?

It may seem too obvious to state, but your first step is to *decide* to become a best-selling published author.

Let's do one thing first, though.

Let's talk about those other co-authored book projects you've participated in that were more nightmare than sweet dreams. And let's talk about that time you dropped $30,000 to write a bestseller that kinda didn't turn out like you thought it would. If this isn't you, then maybe you've just heard horror stories. I've heard them, too!

If you've been an entrepreneur for any length of time, you've undoubtedly been encouraged to create systems and processes. If you already run a highly successful enterprise, you know these, combined with your excellent team, are your lifeblood! Multi-author book projects fail when a non-expert thinks it will be simple to throw content together. Ha!

Think of making a decision with two people about what to eat tonight.

OK, now add one more person, say your mother-in-law, who doesn't like spicy food or noisy places. Now where are you going to eat?

Last assignment—add 20 or 30 people to your living room and decide where to eat, how to get there, and who pays... before you faint from hunger or decide to bail!

Look at it another way.

Statistically, the vast majority of people who buy a course don't complete the course. Is that the fault of the expert who created the course? No! It's human nature to grab at a passing fancy, over-commit, or not ever fully commit. Why would joining a collaborative project with dozens of other people be any different?

The keys to having a successful, rewarding co-authored project—whether you are merely writing one chapter as a participant or you are organizing the effort after your summit or podcast—are to limit the total number of authors, have excellent systems and project management in place to keep things on track, and to carefully vet each person for their commitment to meeting deadlines. Otherwise, people disappear, and the book is months late—if it ever gets published at all. That leaves a really sour taste for anyone who said yes to that project.

If you have participated in an unfortunate project like that, know that you aren't alone. Do your due diligence on the next one. Say YES to the good ones! No point in limiting your future opportunities because of one mismanaged project in the past, right?

Your next step is to decide you are open to removing self-imposed limits.

A book is not defined in just one way. You don't have to stop after producing one kind of book. You don't have to stop just because you already have a book. When you observe the biggest and most influential entrepreneurs, you will see that they often partner to produce content—whether that's books or events. You will note they also have produced more than one book. They view it as a valuable tool for brand authority and lead generation.

The third step is to appreciate that writing a best-selling book is neither hard nor time-consuming. But to do it correctly and produce a product you are proud of, you must be strategic in how you produce it. It's one thing to say it doesn't need to be hard, but it's another to approach it as an afterthought. Write a book that's worth reading, that changes someone's life and business. That's more than a bunch of transcribed words.

Once you've made the decision, produced the work well, and been recognized for its success, and yours, keep the momentum going.

If you aren't working with a PR person already, find one. Public Relations works to expose your brand, but that won't help your business if you don't already have a system to nurture new leads. Luckily for you, you had to make sure all that was in place when you created your book content!

The primary role of your PR team is consistent outreach to various media outlets. Ideally, you want an agency that specializes in media relations and will work on short-term contracts. PR puts your brand top-of-mind with your ideal prospects, so when it comes time to buy, your brand is what they turn to first for help.

If you've decided to increase your following on YouTube or Instagram or even on Facebook, find someone to do it for you or to work with you. Keep building your Rolodex of individuals, teams, or agencies who will keep you out of busy work so you can maintain time with your family, time for growth, and time for strategy. Leave the work outside your core skill set to others who have those things as their superpowers.

Celebrate your accomplishments! Share the news intentionally, so others celebrate with you. And be sure to capitalize on your success and the buzz it generates. It serves no one for you to play small. Go Big! And get key folks in place to make going big a breeze!

WHO: Akbar Sheikh! Case Study Success!

Million Dollar Story Author-Entrepreneur Akbar Sheikh

Let me highlight a member of our Million Dollar Story community. Akbar Sheikh is a #1 International Best-Selling author, speaker, and master of the 7 Ethical Principles of Persuasion. He has helped eight+ funnels hit 7-figures. He is also a father and philanthropist with a concentration on orphans and giving the gift of vision to blind children. He is on a mission to create a massive impact through coaching and believes that as people earn more, they can give more—to their families, communities, and favorite charities—hence, making the world a better place. If you want his help to make more to give more, reach out to him here—**www.AkbarSheikh.com**.

BONUS 1:
YOUR PODCAST BOOK LAUNCH TOUR

BONUS 2:
THE INFLUENCER'S SECRET TO TRAFFIC

"There's a pivotal point when a team becomes a family and when an organization becomes a movement." Robin Arzón, Peloton

WHAT Result Will You Achieve?

Who is Robin Arzón, and why have I used her quotes throughout The Million Dollar Method^{TM}?

Each module in this book shares something she has said that has been heard by hundreds of thousands of people.

She was diagnosed with Type 1 diabetes when she was 33 years old. As of this writing, she is on the Leadership Council of **Beyond Type One**, a nonprofit organization focused on raising awareness about Type 1 Diabetes founded by Nick

Jonas. (I know about Robin because my daughter has T1D and works for BTO and because I ride a Peloton bike.)

Let me give you a timeline…

In 2013 Robin Arzón co-founded the fitness movement *Undo Ordinary* and the print publication *Undo* magazine because she was inspired to show others that there is an alternative way to be an athlete.

In 2014, the same year she was diagnosed with T1D, she joined Peloton in New York City as an instructor.

In 2015, she was one of 20 athletes filmed for a show on National Geographic Channel's, MYGRATIONS. Their path followed the annual spring wildebeest migration journey that begins in the Serengeti Plains and ends at Maasai Mara in Kenya.

In 2016, Robin was promoted to Vice President of Fitness and Programming of Peloton. That same year she was featured in Adidas' campaign *Here to Create* commercial; she is a global Adidas Ambassador.

Also, in 2016 she wrote and published, *Shut Up and Run: How to Get Up, Lace Up, and Sweat with Swagger.*

In 2020, at the age of 39 and as a T1D, she entered the categories of 'geriatric' and 'high risk' for her pregnancy'; she continued to ride and inspire tens of thousands of people daily, especially pregnant women and those with autoimmune disease.

Also in 2020, she was named one of the most influential people on Fortune Magazine's 40 Under 40 list.

In March 2021, she gave birth to a healthy child, Athena—and in June, *she published another book, "Strong Mama"!* Why? Because Influencers know the power of becoming a published author to grow their audience and brand—and a book's power to make a difference and change lives!

WHY Does This Result Matter?

Let's flash back.

In 1981 she was born in Philly to immigrant parents. Her dad is an attorney and former law professor, born in Puerto Rico, and her mom is a physician, born in Cuba.

Her path, she thought, was to follow in her father's footsteps.

In 2000, Robin began her undergraduate studies at New York University.

In 2002, Arzón was taken hostage with 40 others in a wine bar in Manhattan's East Village. "A man, armed with three pistols and a samurai sword, shot three people, doused the group with kerosene, and threatened them with a barbecue lighter. He grabbed Arzon by the hair and held the gun and lighter to her head while using her as a human shield to communicate with the police. Two patrons eventually tackled the man, allowing police to enter the bar and subdue him." [*"How Robin Arzon, a former non-athlete, became the face of fitness for cycling superpower Peloton*." *ESPN.com*. 2019-05-23.]

In 2003 she ran her first mile—ever. It began as a means to deal with trauma. It became her first step towards 'credible authority' in an entirely new-to-her endeavor.

In 2004, she graduated Magna Cum Laude from NYU.

In 2007, she received her JD from Villanova University School of Law. She then spent seven years as a corporate litigator at Paul, Hastings, Janofsky & Walker, LLP.

In 2014, the same year she was diagnosed with T1D, she left a career she was heavily invested in and began a career that would become a movement.

No doubt Robin Arzón is an attractive character and a kick-ass competitor.

She is an Influencer and an inspiration. She makes us believe. She is bold, and her vision is bold. She attracts the company of other big influencers, both people and companies. That fuels her authority and the attention she commands, with more press, more recognition, more respect.

HOW Do You Accomplish This Result?

But what about the rest of us?

I'd like to give you several approaches to getting traffic, attracting attention, growing your authority, and increasing your influence.

One is the Million Dollar Method^{TM}, the theme of this entire book.

When you become a Best-Selling author, you raise your Influence, grow your audience, and generate revenue fast. When you use the process of creating your book to also create all the assets for your business infrastructure in just 90 days, you are strongly positioned to scale your business to $100,000 per month and beyond!

I won't say more—you've read this far. The only action required of you now is to let me know which vehicle you choose to take you to your destination of being a published, best-selling author.

Do you want to hop in the model that helps you write your book as a solo author, but you do so in a cohort of our community members? We either treat this as a fully Done-For-You process, or we guide you through it, coordinating the project so you capitalize on the shared audience reach and collaboration of your colleagues on launch day.

Do you want to catch a ride in the model that has you co-authoring a themed book in health, wealth, or relationships? This is the fastest, easiest path as you utilize our Done-For-You services.

Would you rather catch the group Uber, the shared ride of a Mastermind, where we work together over twelve weeks to scale your business to $100,000 per month? Here you can choose solo-authoring or repurposing your content from summits, podcasts, YouTube Channels, or blogs for your book content. More importantly, we show you how to craft your course or Mastermind in tangent with your chapter outline and set yourself up for traffic and growth. We guide you while you do the majority of the legwork.

Your last entry point headed towards your destination is the DIY monthly membership option. You manage the project at your own pace. This is ideal for you if you have a book you want to re-launch, if you have written most of your new or next book and want to understand better how to publish, launch, and monetize strategically, or if you just don't love working under too much pressure and already have a few other things on your plate.

Recall that if you write the right book strategically, if you choose, you can also craft your course or high-ticket mastermind simultaneously with writing your book. This is a highly efficient process to get business results quickly. You will have both the front-end and back-end funnel assets ready to go.

So how do you get traffic to your offer—whether that's your book or high-ticket course, mastermind, or event?

One powerful method is to do a podcast book tour. Simply reach out to a key handful of community members and ask for the opportunity to be a guest on their show to talk about your new book and offer and how it will get results for their audience. You can even have a special freebie for their audience. Then schedule a show or two per day for a week. You just reached 1000's of new prospects and you never left home!

Another powerful method is to follow a process we use for

organic traffic. In just a few hours per day, or with the help of a VA or appointment setter, you can use excerpts from your book as content and drive people to your funnel and/or to a call with your team.

Not only do we have a proven process and system you can follow, but we also have software that's new to the market and is yielding powerful results. We can show you how to marry the right process with the right tool for fast results without ad spend. The beauty here is that you determine the right message to deliver to the right audience that's ready to receive— and now when you invest in paid traffic your ROA (return on ad spend) will be positive!

You can also follow the route of affiliate marketing where you share rewards without any risk, like our author Eric Beer, who has mastered helping entrepreneurs and brands start and close conversations.

The Million Dollar Method ™ is built for you to work once, invest once, and compound your results into millions—millions of eyeballs and millions in revenue. When you use organic traffic to prove which messaging converts best, you save yourself tens of thousands of dollars in wasted ad spend for ads that don't convert. You use your book to meet all facets of The Profit Pentagon^{TM,} including attracting traffic with solid margins. We don't believe in wasting effort or money!

WHO: Eric Beer! Case Study Success!

Million Dollar Story Author-Entrepreneur Eric Beer

Let me highlight a member of our Million Dollar Story community. Eric Beer is Founder & CEO of Universal Marketing Partners. Serial Entrepreneur, Expert Affiliate Marketer, Lead Generation, and Digital Marketer looking to share his knowledge with the world and add meaning to his efforts. Universal Marketing Partners (UMP) is a global marketing technology company that helps brands "start conversations" and "close conversions." The core of UMP's approach centers on harnessing the power of data collected from marketing activities to then inform the execution of media buying events. By building an ecosystem that integrates actionable data across the product lines, UMP effectively drives a conversation into a conversion and consistently delivers clients outstanding **ROI** results. Eric is also the host of the *Performance Marketing Podcast*.

NEXT STEPS: HOW TO GET MORE HELP

Now it's time for you to invest in yourself.

Reflect on your backstory, why you do what you do, and what has brought you this far.

Close your eyes and dream of the future for a moment. Where is your business headed? Where will your unique abilities and expertise take your prospects and clients? Where will your mission take you? How will the movement you start change lives?

You believe with certainty that you are here to serve and that you have solutions to improve people's lives and businesses. Think about the tactics you teach to help people who are in real pain right now. How can you reach more people? How can you reach them faster?

Think about the people and businesses you have already helped. Isn't that the best feeling ever? You know the world really needs you—needs all of us—right now, don't you?

It's your mission to inspire others to take action and turn big dreams into reality. You do that by leading! Be the example!

Know that most of us thought we were headed one way only to have life throw us one or more curveballs, redirecting our paths significantly. We learned things when that happened, things we are driven to share with others.

Most of us have failed—fallen hard, disappointed ourselves or our family, felt lost, struggled for direction, caused financial stress—and ended up being so much stronger and focused as a result of those experiences. You know someone, somewhere is in the thick of it right now. You can help—they just have to know how to find you fast!

As entrepreneurs, each of us has chosen to forego a paycheck in exchange for living intentionally and deliberately. We are each driven by our desire to make a difference, make an impact, and serve—and to do so has been a scary, uncomfortable, and deliberate choice to grow outside our comfort zones. It feels amazeballs to find our tribe, to work together alongside others who get us. Authoring as part of an entrepreneurial community is a powerful way for us to thrive surrounded by like-minded influencers.

We firmly believe that the more we step into who we are, who we serve, and why, the more our horizons expand, and the more we find ourselves presented with new challenges. What's different for those of us who have become published best-selling authors and wrapped our business offers around our books is that we believe 100% and more that our big ginormous glorious dreams are possible. That *we* are possible!

I believe you are here to serve your readers and clients by using your unique experiences and expertise to offer them immediate relief, hope, and transformation because someone, somewhere, right now, is waiting desperately for YOU to provide a solution to their pain!

Your Million Dollar Story begins with clarity and action. It is your time to act and it is your time to recognize *you are exactly where you are meant to be!*

My wish for you is that the Million Dollar Method™ nourishes your belief, providing you with the courage to keep going in pursuit of your dreams—even if your dreams are forced in a new direction. I invite you to discover how collectively we, as the growing community of Million Dollar Story author-entrepreneurs has already demonstrated, may use our unique stories and gifts, at any age, to change the world in small or large measure.

Entrepreneurs who build movements know we can't do it alone.

Influence requires numbers which is why....

Influencers build networks.

Influencers build audience reach.

Influencers use tools and strategies to go faster.

Action matters—reach out today to get started with the Million Dollar Method^{TM} to grow your influence, audience, and revenue fast!

When you write the right book strategically for your business, you plan to achieve the following results:

An evergreen *Lead Gen/Prospecting* tool

A *Lead Nurture* system so prospects get to Know, Like & Trust you

A *Lead Conversion* system so cold leads are warmed up as they read your book so conversion rates go up and conversion costs go down

A Done For You Business *Client Delivery/Fulfillment* system: Sales Funnel + Assets of free lead magnet, F+S book, Bump Offer, and First OTO (your course or mastermind)

Client Retention and Ascension/Upsell system with a strategically written book bringing clients into your value ladder who become raving lifelong fans

A completed *ebook*

A completed *print book*

A completed *audiobook*

A *Published* book

A *Launched* book

Best Seller status as a published author

A Process to *Monetize* based on your book

BRAND awareness

Elevated *AUTHORITY*

Personal Fulfillment because you DID IT!

You have become a published, best selling author & you have grown your influence, audience, and revenue fast—now you are positioned to start or grow your movement, make a difference, impact lives, and leave your legacy

HOW TO ACCESS YOUR BONUSES

Throughout the book you were given access to several free bonuses. These are training videos, templates, and tools to accompany the content in this book.

While you have already seen the links, here is a list for your quick and easy reference.

1. If you're curious how healthy your Influencer Score is today and want to identify which areas you could improve, take the quick survey here—
   https://www.milliondollarstory.co/ yourinfluencerprofilescorecard

2. I invite you to request to join my free Facebook™ group called the *"Influencer Circle."* It's a group I share with fellow mission-and-success-driven entrepreneurs who are committed to growing their influence,

status, and client base to make a more significant impact and change more lives.

3. The awesome thing is I'm not asking you to create your Dream 100 list where you not only have to research and identify 100 people, but somehow you have to approach them and get them to respond to your ask. You can choose just 2-4 influencers with products and services that add value to your customers, and now you don't have to waste time building an offer that is outside your core competency. You can access my Million Dollar Rolodex here to help you find co-authors, JV or affiliate partners, or folks with skills that will move your business forward fast.
https://www.milliondollarstory.co/mdm-reader-bonus-rolodex

4. Listen to what Peng Joon and Dan Henry say about choosing to become a published author to position your brand authority *https://www.milliondollarstory.co/brand-authority-advice-mdm-reader-bonus*

5. If you want a copy of the Million Dollar Method[TM] Trello board, you can grab that here: *https://www.milliondollarstory.co/trello-board-template-mdm-reader-bonus*

6. If you have expertise and see the merit in becoming a published, best-selling author in an upcoming Million Dollar Story, be sure to get on our waiting

list here: *https://www.milliondollarstory.co/write-that-book-this-year*

7. If you are determined to self-publish, here's a brief video with some how-to pointers for you: *https://www.milliondollarstory.co/self-publish-mdm-reader-bonus*

8. If you want a copy of my free+shipping book funnel, click here. *https://www.milliondollarstory.co/funnel-template-free-plus-shipping-mdm-reader-bonus*

9. Feel free to pick up a copy of the Narration Guide I give my authors so they can produce high quality audiobooks here: *https://www.milliondollarstory.co/audiobook-narration-guide-mdm-reader-bonus*

10. If you want to know more about when to use an ISBN or a Library of Congress number, or how to acquire either, you can watch a short video here. *https://www.milliondollarstory.co/isbn-how-and-when-to-use-one-mdm-reader-bonus*

11. If you want to know how you can easily create author pages, grab my 'How To' guide here so you can link your new book and any other books you have: *https://www.milliondollarstory.co/author-page-creation-mdm-reader-bonus*

If you're ready to become a published, bestselling author fast, even if you don't like to write or don't have time, we have solutions!

JOIN our FREE group, grab your FREE book, & check your Influencer Score for FREE!

Influencer Circle Community—Ask To Join US!
https://www.facebook.com/groups/
influencercircle.milliondollarstory

What Is YOUR Influencer Score?
Find Out If Your Influence Is As Healthy As You Hope It Is & Where It Might Need A Boost!

Find Your Grade Here:
https://www.milliondollarstory.co/
yourinfluencerprofilescorecard

SPEAK TO US

Ready To Become A Published Best-Selling Author Without Writing A Word Or Getting **Distracted From Your Core Business?**

If you would like help from my team using our Done-For-You services to solo author a book and create your next offer, know that it is best to book a call so that we understand your area of expertise.

You may want to co-author in a collaborative work with other influencers so you only have to write one chapter. Be sure to reserve a spot in the next book that complements your topic so that we can select the best influencers for you to partner with to grow your list, audience reach, and impact.

If you are looking to participate in our Done-With-You Masterclass to scale your business to $100,000 per month and beyond, these are offered four times per year. It's best to reserve early. And if you want to know more about our monthly membership offer with no contract or long-term commitment, just ask.

We can't wait to speak with you and support you in becoming a published, best-selling author this year so that you grow your influence, audience, and revenue fast!

Book A FREE Call Today!
https://www.milliondollarstory.co/mdm-books-build-businesses

ABOUT THE AUTHOR— JAMIE WOLF

Photo by John Arthur Photography

I'm Jamie Wolf.

I help experts write best-selling books and I help entrepreneurs use those books to build their brand and authority and scale their business to $100,000 per month and beyond.

I help YOU become a best-selling author!

I help your BUSINESS thrive and scale faster!

My Agency can create, publish, and market your ebook, print book, and audiobook FOR you.

We can do that WITH you, especially when we work together to not only craft your book but also to create all assets for your business infrastructure while driving traffic to your offers fast.

Or I can give you the training to do it by yourself.

I am the CEO and President of Million Dollar Story Agency, a multiple best-selling author, and the owner of a boutique imprint, Wolf Tide Publishing.

100% of the entrepreneurs I've worked with have become Amazon Best Selling published authors—in 90 days or less without even writing—and have stayed in the Top 100 in multiple categories for twelve or more months.

Even if you have NOT thought of writing a book because you are too busy growing your business, I invite you to think strategically and be as efficient as possible with your resources of time, money, energy, focus, and fulfillment.

Rather than think of a book as the endpoint, think of the exercise of writing a book as one that brings your ideal customer and the result you deliver to them or for them into crystal clear focus. Recognize a book as a vehicle that picks up cold traffic and delivers it to you as warm traffic, ready to buy from you because after consuming your stories, your prospects now relate to you and see themselves in your journey; they believe you can and will help them.

Finally, conserve your time and energy by crafting your book and course or mastermind simultaneously in order to build out your entire business infrastructure of front-end and back-end offers once, within 90 days, while creating the systems and process to master organic traffic and team building. Get out of overwhelm and busyness and scale your business to $100,000 per month and beyond!

If you want to boost your status, easily attract new customers, make more sales, position yourself as an authority quickly, and warrant premium pricing —even if you feel you are too busy or don't like to write—we have a unique proprietary system to get you results fast.

If the thought of writing a book keeps surfacing but you aren't sure how to start (or finish), I invite you to join my free Face-book^{TM} group called the *"Influencer Circle."* It's a group I share with fellow mission-and-success-driven entrepreneurs who are committed to growing their influence, status, and client base to make a more significant impact and change more lives.

If you've rarely thought of becoming an author, but you are

driven to scale your business to profit so you can make a bigger difference for yourself, your family, your community, and those you serve, the Million Dollar Method^{TM} is your solution to consistent and fast growth and impact.

I know you have a story and solutions worth sharing!

I believe that when you realize it's fully possible to scale your business to $100,000 per month and beyond, you will embrace the true legacy you are here to make. The Million Dollar Method^{TM} takes away the complexity and overwhelm, and gets you to results with relentless focus so you stop drowning in your business and get to doing what you love most, changing lives now.

I have been fortunate enough to have a long and varied professional journey, having worked extensively in science and business. I merged the two fields when I co-founded a medical tech and disease management company that got a product through FDA clearance in less than two years while raising millions of dollars.

I hold an MBA from Arizona State University and over a lifetime of work—so far—I've experienced the roles of student, employee, corporate management, consultant, tech start-up co-founder, syndicated columnist, author, publisher, real estate investor, and owner of a boxing gym. What emerged from those experiences is a passion for working with success-and-mission-driven entrepreneurs to help them tell their stories and significantly grow their revenue, influence, and impact.

I'm also the host of a podcast, **Million Dollar PIVOT** where I interview entrepreneurs with stories to share that will help you believe *you've got this!*

I am a mom of three adult kids, a lifelong rescuer of critters, and an eternal optimist both despite and because of life and the lessons it has thrown at me. I adore business because problem solving fascinates me. I believe we each have unrealized potential for greatness and for giving back to the world that gives us so much.

I am also a fierce advocate for people and their stories. I am here to share *your* stories so you can grow your influence, audience, and revenue fast. If you're ready to write a Best Selling book to become a Best Selling author to scale your business to $100,000 per month and beyond, reach me here **https://www.MillionDollarStory.co** or schedule your free strategy call without delay. **https://calendly.com/milliondollarstory/influencer-circle-scale-your-business**

Don't delay. I currently have a waiting list for both our

Do-It-Together Mastermind program and our Done-For-You services. Be sure to join the Facebook group and schedule a call today!

**NOW IT'S TIME TO SHARE *YOUR* STORY &
SCALE YOUR BUSINESS!**
**Become a bestselling author, scale your business, &
significantly**
GROW YOUR INFLUENCE, AUDIENCE, & REVENUE
FAST!

We know how busy you are so let us help you simultaneously
write your story, craft your course, & **build out your
business infrastructure** *in the next three months* so you can
get to doing what you love most -
help your clients and make a difference!

Do it ***TODAY***
Go to:
http://milliondollarstory.co
**People are waiting to hear your story...
it's time for you to share it!**

WE HAVE A BIG FAVOR TO ASK – WILL YOU HELP US?

Thank You For Reading *Million Dollar Method*^{TM}!

I really appreciate your feedback, and I love hearing your ideas about the book and how you relate to these stories—and how you are taking action! The team at Million Dollar Story Agency wants to know that the stories we tell and we produce are making a difference!

Please go to Amazon today and share your thoughts about the book. We appreciate your time and feedback *ginormously*!

Thanks again!
~ Jamie Wolf

Made in the USA
Monee, IL
07 October 2022

15408741R00138